Invite · Welcome · Connect

stories & tools to transform your church

© 2018 Forward Movement
Third printing, 2019

ISBN 978-0-88028-461-5

Printed in the USA

Forward
Movement
inspire disciples. empower evangelists.

Invite · Welcome · Connect

stories & tools to transform your church

MARY FOSTER PARMER

FORWARD MOVEMENT
Cincinnati, Ohio

To my grandson Ike, my inspiration for this ministry

Contents

Foreword

Brothers and sisters,

You are about to embark on a journey of Invite Welcome Connect, a ministry designed to help Episcopalians engage in the deep work of evangelism. How do we define evangelism? I think Mary Parmer and her ministry of Invite Welcome Connect have given us a way forward.

As Episcopalians, we are not God's frozen. We are God's introverted people. We tend to be shy and polite. We are not pushy people—that's not our way. And I don't think we need to pretend to be that way. We need to be who we are. Mary Parmer has found a way for God to guide people in sharing their stories in ways that are authentic and genuine.

I participated in this program as the bishop of North Carolina, and our diocese was very involved in this ministry. Invite Welcome Connect is a wonderful program, but it's more than simply a program: It helps to inculcate a way of life that actually reflects the way of welcome of Jesus of Nazareth, the Jesus who says, "Come unto me all ye who are weary and heavy laden, and I will give you rest." Invite Welcome Connect is something we as Episcopalians can do. It's a way of evangelism that reflects who we are, that doesn't have us trying to be somebody we aren't, but actually calls us to be exactly who we are in Jesus Christ, and to invite, and welcome, and connect others to that life-giving reality.

In this book, Mary shares the deep truths of Invite Welcome Connect, rooted in the gospel and in our tradition as followers of Christ. I encourage all Episcopalians to embrace Invite Welcome Connect as one way to live into the Jesus Movement.

God bless you, God keep you, and let's keep this Jesus Movement going.

> Michael B. Curry
> XXVII Presiding Bishop
> The Episcopal Church

Introduction

All creativity is discovery: creating is discovering something you did not know before which has sprung from the things you know very well.

Willie Morris, *My Mississippi*

These words by southern writer Willie Morris speak to the birthing of Invite Welcome Connect. The creation of this ministry originated at a deep level from my own experiences and personal faith journey, things I knew well as a child of storytellers and Southern hospitality. The creation of this ministry also stemmed from the faith stories of hundreds of fellow Episcopalians who love this beloved church as I do.

The discovery of what I "did not know before" came as I developed the initial newcomer process some twenty years ago. What I discovered then and continue to encounter is that Episcopalians are good at knowing the words of the creeds, Baptismal Covenant, and many of the hallmark stories of scripture. But when it comes to living out the Baptismal Covenant and incarnational theology, we are oftentimes tongue-tied and helpless. We know how to be gracious and hospitable—and we can throw a good party! We are aware, on an intellectual level, that God created and endowed each of us with gifts and talents. But where we struggle is in sharing this faith. Most Episcopalians are not comfortable inviting people to church. As a denomination, we have no clue how to share our faith story. We recite the motto of "The Episcopal Church Welcomes You," but we don't know how (or are unwilling) to make that a reality. Many Episcopalians do not know how to discern the deep well of gifts and talents given to them individually, nor do they understand the importance of creativity and relational ministry in congregational development.

This discovery has become the foundation of Invite Welcome Connect. For our congregations to thrive—spiritually and numerically—we need more than a newcomer ministry. For us to live into God's call to share the good news of Christ far and wide, to serve the poor, and to love our neighbors, we need a ministry that is deeper and wider than we have imagined, that not only invites and welcomes visitors but also works to fully incorporate them into the body of Christ.

This book tells the story of the creation and growth of the ministry we know today as Invite Welcome Connect and many of the ways it has inspired and transformed people and communities across the church. Designed for individuals, small groups, and congregations, this book explores the basic structure of Invite Welcome Connect and its theological underpinnings and offers questions for reflection and some initial ideas to spur your own creative solutions based on context and need. There's plenty of white space in the margins to take notes, jot down ideas, or doodle! The appendix includes a basic getting started guide for launching your own Invite Welcome Connect ministry as well as additional tools, and I encourage you to visit the website, www.invitewelcomeconnect.sewanee.edu for more resources. The Invite Welcome Connect team is also available for workshops and conferences. And of course, at the heart of this ministry and this book are stories and tools from clergy and lay leaders across the church who have implemented Invite Welcome Connect in their congregations and experienced blessed transformation.

During my recent recovery from surgery, I found myself binge-watching the TV show, *Fixer Upper*, where a couple from Waco, Texas, help folks find and renovate houses, some of which are in a total state of disrepair. The hosts, Chip and Joanna, often ask the question, "Do you have the guts to take on a fixer-upper?" It occurred to me during one of the episodes that this might be an apt question for the Episcopal Church today. We are at yet another crossroads in the life of this beloved church: Some people hold the opinion that we are in a state of irreparable, hopeless decline. But others, including me, believe there is great promise and hope for our church—along with significant work!

My challenge and invitation to those of us who love the church is to ask ourselves the question, "Do we have the guts to take on this fixer-upper?" Either we live fearlessly into who we proclaim to be—the Episcopal Branch of the Jesus Movement—or we wallow and hand-wring, enslaved by the sins of despair, complacency, and fear. We either intentionally step out in faith, imagining the limitless possibilities for our congregations, no matter the size, or we continue in a state of hopeless decline and disarray. I believe we can change the negative narrative of despair and hopelessness, but it will take courageous, hopeful leaders who are willing to do what it takes—who have the guts—to implement the essentials of Invite Welcome Connect. I invite you to join us on this journey of transformation.

Mary Foster Parmer
The Feast of Pentecost

Chapter 1

THE STORY

The power of story is at the heart of this work, and I will start with mine.

Born in Brookhaven and raised in Natchez, Mississippi, I am the middle of five children of Southern Baptist parents. I was blessed with a family who understood the importance of the deeply Southern gift of hospitality. Visiting pastors and missionaries to Riverside Baptist Church often stayed in our home, and there seemed to be a continuous flow of friends, family, and even strangers. This relational gift, ingrained in me at a young age, was the seed of the ministry God would call me to many years later.

I went to Mississippi State for two years, got married, had two children, divorced after twenty years, and then opened a physician-recruiting firm in Beaumont, Texas. Sitting in my office in downtown Beaumont in the fall of 1995, I received a call from Sally Dooley, with whom I sat on various community boards. Sally invited me to her church, St. Mark's Episcopal in Beaumont, and I accepted her invitation not only out of respect for her but also out of curiosity about this faith tradition she so obviously loved.

Attending St. Mark's Episcopal Church was my first experience of worship in a liturgical church, and I was completely overwhelmed. In retrospect, I realize I had no idea what "liturgy" meant, but at the time it was clear I was in the midst of the most Holy, and my soul was touched in a way that to this day is hard to describe. I was drawn to the reverence, the spoken word, the music, the prayers, and especially the simple act of kneeling with others in the congregation.

Throughout the following year, I struggled with what I now know was a call from God. I spent hours reading, journaling, taking long hikes, meditating, praying, and soul searching, and I envisioned a life of purpose, happiness, and healing for myself. Weir Smith, a licensed family therapist who happened to be Episcopalian, was instrumental in bringing me along to a place of emotional and spiritual healing.

What would my Southern Baptist family think? How would I earn a living if I said yes to God's call in my life?

I had been seeing Weir prior to my first visit to St. Mark's, and she encouraged me to read books that opened me up to an unfamiliar world of thought: Henri Nouwen's *Reaching Out*, Joseph Campbell's *The Power of Myth*, and Hannah Hurnard's *Hinds Feet on High Places*. I had a deep, intuitive sense that God was calling me to ministry, but fear prevented me from taking action. What would my Southern Baptist family think? How would I earn a living if I said yes to God's call in my life?

In the summer of 1996, I was at a committee meeting for Young Life, an organization that supports and encourages teens in their faith, and the group leader, Don Joseph, invited me to his church, St. Stephen's Episcopal Church, Beaumont. Don said he thought I would like the new rector because he was a Southerner like me. On Sunday, August 16, I walked up the long sidewalk to the doors of St. Stephen's, and I met the Rev. Patrick Gahan. It didn't take me long to know that this was my spiritual home. Within a few months, I was confirmed. Coming from the Southern Baptist faith tradition, I had a lot of questions. Patrick listened and answered and let me explore my concerns.

The Episcopal Church is indeed a big umbrella, holding many varying opinions and theological stances, he explained. But at the same time, Episcopalians are bound together by their common belief in Jesus, holy scripture, *The Book of Common Prayer*, and the creeds. I began to answer God's call. I closed my business and accepted a position as director of adult ministries and evangelism. Little did I know what else God had in store for me!

In 2007, I moved to Austin and attended St. Edward's University full time, graduating *summa cum laude* with a bachelor's degree in religious studies. Given that I thoroughly enjoyed the intellectual stimulation of researching, writing, and publishing theological articles while at St. Edward's, I began investigating avenues for further studies. But the idea of continuing my education took a back seat when, in 2009, I received an invitation from Claude E. Payne, retired bishop of the Diocese of Texas, to become the first director of a new initiative called the Gathering of Leaders, a national leadership group for young Episcopal clergy. I accepted Bishop Payne's invitation immediately, with the realization that God works in mysterious ways. Back in 1995, Sally Dooley invited me to go to church with her because she had attended a large diocesan gathering where newly elected Bishop Payne cast his vision for the diocese to move from maintenance to mission. He challenged everyone at the gathering to go home and invite someone to church. Sally, an introvert, was simply doing what her bishop told her to do.

BIRTHING THE MINISTRY

I served for ten years at St. Stephen's, Beaumont, learning from Patrick Gahan as he modeled the importance of relational parish ministry and empowering laity for ministry. St. Stephen's was Patrick's first church as rector, and he decided to intentionally implement Bishop Payne's missionary vision. Patrick was unflinching and relentless in implementing this vision to move the parish out of maintenance mode into a parish of a mission of transformation. We began creating and developing a model for newcomer ministry that revolved around welcoming visitors and following up with them. Within three years, the changes in our faith community were dramatic. The average Sunday attendance more than doubled from 121 to 325, choir membership quadrupled, vacation Bible school attendance tripled, and the church's mean membership age dropped by ten years. The congregation built a temporary building to house overflowing children's programs. In 2000, the Rev. Canon Kevin Martin, then canon for congregational development for the diocese, invited a team from St. Stephen's to share stories about the growth of our church at a Diocese of Texas conference, and we introduced for the first time the core content of our newcomer process. As word spread throughout the Diocese of

Texas about the efficacy of this newcomer ministry process, we began receiving requests to give presentations at various clergy and lay leadership events.

For congregational leadership presentation purposes, I initially named this newcomer process "Sacred Connection," and after a few years I changed it to Invitation, Welcome, Connection. In 2010, Andy Doyle, the Diocese of Texas's new bishop, and Mary MacGregor, director of congregational development and evangelism, invited me to further develop this newcomer process and explore whether the model that had been so successful at St. Stephen's could be replicated and implemented in other places. Three Diocese of Texas churches were assigned as pilot congregations for this effort, and a fourth congregation asked to be a part of what I subsequently named the Newcomer Ministry Project. As I worked with the four pilot congregations to develop checklists and resources, we began offering workshops at the diocesan centers in Houston and Austin. The stories, experiences, and feedback gleaned from clergy and lay leaders at these workshops were invaluable as I continued to refine and update the core content.

The churches involved in the program reported immediate numerical growth, and the project spread to more than 100 congregations in the Diocese of Texas over the next three years. In addition to a growth in numbers, the congregations reported a renewed sense of energy and enthusiasm in their parishioners.

TAKING FLIGHT

In April 2013, the Rev. Frank Allen, a Gathering of Leaders member, invited me to bring the Invitation Welcome Connection ministry to his congregation, St. David's Episcopal Church in Wayne, Pennsylvania. I led a workshop for St. David's clergy and lay leaders, along with a number of other leaders from congregations in the dioceses of Pennsylvania and Bethlehem. Word spread quickly, and invitations from around the country began arriving. Another priest and Gathering of Leaders member, the Rev. Justin Lindstrom, suggested I rename the work: Invite Welcome Connect. These action words were perfect, speaking to the heart of the ministry.

The first national Invite Welcome Connect Summit was sponsored by the Diocese of Texas and held at the Episcopal conference center, Camp Allen, in April 2015. Michael B. Curry, then bishop of the Diocese of North Carolina, preached at the opening service. When Bishop Curry was elected presiding bishop of the Episcopal Church in July 2015, he invited me to keynote the Diocese of North Carolina's 200th Annual Diocesan Convention held that November.

In April 2016, the second national summit was held again at Camp Allen. Plenary and workshop speakers featured clergy and lay leaders from around the country who had embraced and implemented Invite Welcome Connect in their congregations. This second summit bore witness to the viral quality of the practices of Invite Welcome Connect across the Episcopal Church. By this time, I had taken the ministry to thirty-nine dioceses of the Episcopal Church, two Episcopal seminaries, University of Texas and Texas A&M college missioners, and the Anglican Diocese of Calgary. This widespread hunger to learn more about Invite Welcome Connect further convinced me that this was a ministry of and to the whole church.

NEXT STEPS ON THE JOURNEY

I had been praying and pondering about the next steps for Invite Welcome Connect. I wanted this ministry to be rooted in a church-wide organization. While the Diocese of Texas had planted the seeds and supported the early years of Invite Welcome Connect, I had a deep intuitive feeling that this ministry needed to move to a new place. I mentioned this desire to Bishop Duncan Gray of Mississippi. His immediate response: "Have you heard of the Beecken Center at Sewanee?" Bishop Gray told me that along with serving as the administrative location for EfM (Education for Ministry), the Beecken Center was the home for creative ministries such as the Summa Theological Debate Camp for high school students. The first time I looked at the website for the Beecken Center, I had an immediate visceral reaction as the words "Imagine" and "Create" scrolled by, and I saw photos of brainstorming sessions and bright-colored Post-it notes papering walls. These are the very words and tools I use in facilitating Invite Welcome Connect workshops. It felt like this could be home.

I began conversations with the leadership of the University of the South and the Beecken Center, including Bishop J. Neil Alexander, School of Theology dean, and Dr. Courtney Cowart, Beecken Center's executive director. In May 2016, I visited Sewanee for the first time, where I was introduced to the Beecken Center staff. In my journal, I wrote, "For many years I drove from Texas to my hometown, Natchez, Mississippi, through the middle section of Louisiana, and as I crossed over the Mississippi River Bridge, there was a billboard that read, "Mississippi—it's like coming home." These were my sentiments at that first visit to Sewanee, and I continue to feel this way whenever I drive through the campus: "Sewanee—it's like coming home."

A LITTLE HELP FROM FRIENDS

More than a decade ago, Bishop Payne gathered a group of bishops, priests, and lay leaders to begin a conversation about how the Episcopal Church might find renewal and revitalization through a clearer focus on mission and evangelism. This diverse group, inspired by Bishop Payne's vision and hope-filled approach even in the midst of the church's deep division and spiritual fatigue, developed an initiative that is now known as the Gathering of Leaders, a peer-led, invitation-only leadership group for young Episcopal clergy. Today, there are more than 500 participating Gathering of Leaders clergy, including bishops, diocesan staff, seminary deans, and school chaplains.

As I shared earlier, Bishop Payne hired me as the first executive director in 2009. Almost immediately I experienced an extraordinary amount of synergy between the Gathering of Leaders and Invite Welcome Connect. Gathering of Leaders participants are laser-focused on issues of mission, ministry, and evangelism. Early on, many of these clergy became the first people to invite me to share the work of Invite Welcome Connect in their churches and dioceses. The rich conversations during the presentations and at Gathering of Leaders meetings helped shape Invite Welcome Connect. The Gathering of Leaders is purposefully comprised of a variety of clergy who hold differing theological perspectives. Respect for differences and the importance of peer learning are fundamental precepts of the group and helped guide me as I defined the core values of the ministry of Invite Welcome Connect.

Bishop Payne's endorsement for this work is a powerful one, as he imagines what Invite Welcome Connect could become if the church wholeheartedly embraces it.

> The **Invite Welcome Connect** ministry is a theological and practical initiative, which goes beyond making "The Episcopal Church Welcomes You" a reality but also ensures those who do come to faith in our churches do not leave by the back door. It provides a theological rationale for outreach to the spiritually hungry, a means of engaging those who come into our places of worship, and a way to engage those who become a part of our community of faith.
>
> If an Altar Guild can beautifully and habitually attract a dedicated core of hardworking volunteers to tend the sanctuary, similarly organized teams of well-trained laity can welcome seekers and incorporate the newly initiated into our faith communities. Simultaneously the vision of an outward focus can be preached as central to the gospel to encourage congregations to be welcoming and inviting.

Invite Welcome Connect is a model that makes "The Episcopal Church Welcomes You" a reality and not an oxymoron.

— Claude E. Payne

> The Episcopal Church will continue to wallow in a high-maintenance mode until it takes its outreach to seekers as seriously and happily as it does tending the altar. Invite Welcome Connect is a model that makes "The Episcopal Church Welcomes You" a reality and not an oxymoron. Like the Altar Guild, choir, Christian formation ministry, youth ministry, acolytes, lay eucharistic ministers, etc.,

Invite Welcome Connect is a crucial and exciting vehicle for the faithful to fulfill their ministries of being the church.

WHAT IS INVITE WELCOME CONNECT?

Invite Welcome Connect is a ministry of transformation that equips and empowers congregations and individuals to cultivate intentional practices of evangelism, hospitality, and connectedness rooted in the gospel directive to "Go and make disciples of all nations" (Matthew 28:19). The work accommodates congregations of all sizes and socioeconomic situations. The assessment tools, surveys, checklists, and other materials are designed to be adapted based on the interests and needs of a particular locale.

Various attempts to define this ministry have emerged, including the following: a method; a way of imagining evangelism and newcomer ministry; a framework; a process; a creative place where imagination can fly; a gospel imperative. I remain steadfast: Invite Welcome Connect is not a program, nor is it a magic pill for church growth. In the early years of developing this ministry, I had lunch with a rector of a large parish in Texas, and his response to my description of this ministry was, "Mary, rectors at churches the size of mine do not want a program peddled to them." I've decided God has a sense of humor, since the ministry is now one of the "programs" of the Beecken Center at the School of Theology in Sewanee! Nevertheless, I never refer to Invite Welcome Connect as a program but rather as a ministry, a response to God's call to love others and boldly share the good news of the risen Christ.

For many of us, talking about our faith and our church is one of the most difficult things we can do. But what if there was a way to learn and practice in a supportive, non-threatening environment? This is what Invite Welcome Connect does. Mary Parmer has created this extraordinary combination of ideas and life experience. I first met Mary years ago in Austin, Texas, when I was in seminary. I was drawn to Mary's passion for helping congregations understand the importance of personal invitation, welcoming folks, hearing their story, recognizing their gifts, and then connecting them to ministry. This is the essence of living into our Baptismal Covenant!

Invite Welcome Connect is not a program, but a ministry based in scripture, theology, and experience. It is an *ethos*, a way of being. It is comprehensive and incredibly well thought out, but perhaps most importantly, it's exciting! This ministry encourages intentional listening by both the congregation and its individual members. It invites us to hear the story that each person carries, and in listening, acknowledge a deeper bond in Christ and each other.

I firmly believe that every visitor who crosses the threshold of our churches does so by the invitation of the Holy Spirit. In talking with our visitors, I have been told many stories about how that person "just felt like she should come to our church" or "I drove by your church every day on my way to work for five years and never noticed it, but then I just saw it and felt I should visit." We have a responsibility to honor these holy invitations by welcoming, inviting, and connecting each person to the body of Christ, the church.

But this doesn't happen by accident. It happens by cultivating an ethos of Invite Welcome Connect through teaching, prayer, and preaching. It requires training and having parishioners poised and ready with systems in place. And it requires accountability and measuring our metrics to see how we're doing. Since we began implementing the principles of Invite Welcome Connect seven years ago, we have experienced a 22 percent increase in communicants in good standing (1,168 from 957); a 48 percent increase in average Sunday attendance (509 from 337); and a 359 percent increase in "others who are active" (445 from 97) (all numbers from 2017 and 2010 parochial reports). For me the category of "others who are active" is the most significant because these people are in the process of taking the next steps in their spiritual journey at Christ Church Cathedral. The end result is changed lives and vibrant churches.

Brent A. Owens
Associate Dean, Christ Church Cathedral
Lexington, Kentucky

Another way to consider Invite Welcome Connect is through the lens of the three-legged stool of Anglican authority: scripture, tradition, and reason. Based on the theology of Richard Hooker (c. 1554-1600), each source of authority must be perceived in light of the other two. This concept is helpful when exploring the ministry of Invite Welcome Connect: Each of the three components is connected, and transformation will only happen when we intentionally address all three of these essentials. As we live into these practices that will move us from maintenance to mission, we are transformed. Just as the sacraments are outward and visible signs of inward and invisible grace, the action steps of Invite Welcome Connect are outward and visible signs. The inward and spiritual grace is the deeper, inner truth of people's connection with Christ and with the world. This is where real transformation occurs.

A three-legged stool is totally dependent on all three legs. Take one away, you fall. Our success with the Invite Welcome Connect ministry is based on the belief that each of these three aspects is equally important in building a strong, vibrant relationship with each other and the faith community.

To build a stool that is lasting and substantial, there must be a plan. Each of the legs of our stool needed a carpenter—a chairperson—who had a clear understanding of the ministry essentials. In January 2016, we first reached out to and recruited active members of the congregation to work as a unified team committed to opening doors and hearts to anyone seeking to find a place at God's table. All chairs and co-chairs of each team studied the Invite Welcome Connect philosophy and suggestions on how to start. Next each chair (carpenter) built a team with six to ten individuals.

To give ourselves a clear understanding of our goals and objectives, we, with direction from clergy, developed a fluid flowchart, a visual schematic identifying outcomes and illustrating the path from a newcomer's initial contact with the church until that person establishes a meaningful, comfortable place in the St. John's family. Being a fluid instrument, our flowchart has changed over time but always provides sign posts to keep us focused on the journey.

The next step was to have our church family buy into the program. We first introduced the ministry to members in a newsletter article and from the pulpit. People were curious and started asking questions. In July 2016, on three consecutive Sundays, each committee hosted a forum, sharing the philosophy of the essentials along with goals. An underlying message from every team was the importance of each member of the church to the success of the ministry. We included a question-and-answer session. We were learning and growing together.

We held an Invitation Sunday in September 2016, an occasion where each member was encouraged to invite someone to worship, a reception, and tour of the facilities. Because many Episcopalians shy away from the word evangelism, the Invite Committee, with the support of Welcome and Connect, presented an informative, humorous forum on "how to invite" another person to church. What a huge success! Among other initiatives, Invite was tasked with developing a list of "invite friendly" events held each year by the church and encouraged invitations be extended as a way to open the door to others.

Welcome's "Holy Hospitality" is a three-fold ministry. It encompasses the greeters, the ushers, and the distribution of welcome bags from the staffed Welcome Table.

The ushers and the greeters work in conjunction with those at the Welcome Table to identify and welcome new people. Greeters, who wear a greeter tag as well as a name tag, greet individuals, introduce them to other parishioners and clergy, give them a Welcome Bag, and make sure they are escorted to the parish hall for coffee and conversation. They introduce them to at least one other person so that when the visitors come back, they will be able to call at least a few people by their names. We want no stranger in our midst.

Connect's goals are to help identify newcomers' talents and passions by getting to know them as individuals and letting them know that they are needed and vital to St. John's family and the community. Connect's flowchart identifies goals from the first month of contact through the sixth month—from the time newcomers fill out a visitor's card to the time when they (hopefully) feel like they truly belong.

In March 2017, another Invite Welcome Connect forum was held, and two of the new church members spoke about why they had chosen to become a part of the St. John's family. Each had immediately been greeted and felt welcomed and valued at St. John's. Their spiritual and community needs were being met. Their testimonies were proof that Invite Welcome Connect is effective.

This three-legged stool that we have built together has helped guarantee a safe, nurturing place at God's table. The congregation and clergy are the glue that ensures each person has a place among our St. John's family.

Mary Lee Robertson
Lay Leader, St. John's Episcopal Church
Tallahassee, Florida

VISION

The vision of Invite Welcome Connect is to change the culture of the Episcopal Church to move from maintenance to mission. In his seminal book *Culture Making,* author Andy Crouch describes culture as what we make of the world, and he encourages Christians to be creative culture makers. He writes, "If God is at work in every sphere and scale of human culture, then such supernaturally abundant results are potentially present whenever we take the risk of creating a new cultural good... Culture—making something of the world, moving the horizons of possibility and impossibility—is what human beings do and are meant to do. Transformed culture is at the heart of God's mission in the world, and it is the call of God's redeemed people."

Attempting to change the cultures and contexts of individual congregations is not the intent of the Invite Welcome Connect ministry; rather, the vision for this work is to assist communities in becoming creative culture change-makers, moving communities of faith from maintenance to mission. Bishop Claude E. Payne and Hamilton Beazley articulated the difference between the two in their classic book, *Reclaiming the Great Commission*: "The missionary church is forever in deep water, always at risk, continually taking chances as it tries to carry the gospel to the unchurched, in words and ways they can understand. It is the maintenance church that keeps its feet on the shore—unwilling to risk, unwilling to change, unwilling to encounter God in the deep water of the unchurched. Just washing its nets."

> Transformed culture is at the heart of God's mission in the world, and it is the call of God's redeemed people.
>
> – Andy Crouch

Jesus calls us to be fishers of people. Invite Welcome Connect has helped St. John's move from line-catching to building a net for newcomer incorporation. Through the Invite Welcome Connect model, we now think holistically.

Let's begin with the terminology: the genius of this model is that is takes words that are scary to most Episcopalians, words like evangelism and radical hospitality, and replaces them with words that people grasp immediately in or outside of the church: Invite Welcome Connect.

I frame it like this: Every Sunday, Jesus throws a party at church. He is the host, we're all guests, but in our case, we are guests who have already experienced Jesus' welcome. Now, we are to share it with others.

First, we are encouraged to invite people to the party. When we are excited about our faith in God, it's not hard to want others to have the same experience. It's pure joy. In recent years, we've held an Invitation Sunday in the fall. We send out a letter in the summer and ask members to invite someone to church with them. The letter includes practical pointers and is written with a light touch—evangelism doesn't have to be ponderous! We also include Invitation Cards (the size of business cards) with basic information about worship service times, website, social media, parking, and directions that members can give to people they invite.

Second, once folks knock on our door, we open it wide. Our goal is to make visitors feel like they are the most important people in the world to God (which they are!). This is the vital ministry of our greeters, ushers, and Welcome Table volunteers. Invite Welcome Connect has inspired us to revitalize these crucial ministries.

Third, once folks have been welcomed, we introduce them to their fellow guests and make them feel at home. Connect is a particular area on which we needed to concentrate. I personally witnessed many of our newcomers leaving the party through the back door. They would be active for six months and then disappear. Through Invite Welcome Connect, we are now much more intentional about connecting new people to other members and ministries. At the same time, we realize people connect at their own paces. I've witnessed newcomers joining the choir on their very first day with us, and others who need to sit in the back of the church for a year before they get involved with anything. Members of our Connect team are good listeners and appreciate the need for discerning the best approach for each individual.

Last year alone, we welcomed more than 100 new members, all of whom have become meaningfully connected to the St. John's community. I am very excited to see how Invite Welcome Connect will continue to help St. John's grow in numbers and spiritual depth in the future!

David C. Killeen
Rector, St. John's Episcopal Church
Tallahassee, Florida

CORE VALUES

Critical core values undergird Invite Welcome Connect, and participating congregations and those carrying out this work are reminded to keep these values at the forefront of ministry.

PRAYERFUL: We pray God will give us courage to implement the essentials of Invite Welcome Connect in our congregations. We also pray for our hearts to reflect God's gracious invitation and welcome. It is not our table to which we welcome people—it is God's table! One would assume our faith communities are naturally open to welcoming the strangers in their midst; however, this is not always the case. Early on in my travels around the country with this ministry, one vestry member at a small parish told the assembled group she liked the church the size that it was. I am confident that this mindset, fairly typical in many congregations, can be changed through prayer and serious reflection on the alternatives!

The power of one's mindset is explored in Stanford University psychologist Carol S. Dweck's brilliant book, *Mindset: The New Psychology of Success*. People with a fixed mindset are less likely to flourish than those with a growth mindset, and it is important to remember that our mindsets can be changed. Dweck believes people with a fixed mindset rarely push themselves out of their comfort zone for fear of failing or making mistakes, yet those with a growth mindset thrive on challenge and are open to learning and creating, even when things are not going well. This well-documented research is applicable with individuals and businesses alike, so it gives me great hope that the fixed mindsets of many in our faith communities have the ability to be transformed and changed into creative growth mindsets!

> Inattention to the little things leads to the gradual loss of the larger ones.
>
> – Sam Portaro

INTENTIONAL: Living into our Baptismal Covenant is a lifelong process, and it begins with prayerful intentionality and a conscious decision to become reflections of Christ in our actions and reactions to life. We must also intentionally nurture a commitment to implementing the ministry of Invite Welcome Connect, and we do this by organizing the work in a systematic, creative way. The Invite Welcome Connect assessments, checklists, and ideas/resources pages are detailed and process-oriented, and intentionality is crucial in implementing this ministry in our congregations. I remind folks that "God is in the details" with this work, and I offer a quote from Sam Portaro's book, *Brightest and Best*, "Inattention to the little things leads to the gradual loss of the larger ones." For clergy who are averse to detailed, process-oriented work, I strongly suggest they have folks assisting them who have those gifts.

An email I received from a young associate priest illustrates the value of intentionality within this ministry. He attended an Invite Welcome Connect workshop and expressed his concern that as an associate, he would not have the authority to implement the work of Invite Welcome Connect in his parish. I suggested he simply focus his personal energies on individual relationships, inviting, welcoming, and connecting individuals to the Body of Christ. On the Sunday following the workshop he preached about God's desire for us to be in relationship — with God and with one another. He writes, "I ended with an invitation, maybe an exhortation, to relationship. In addition to the general invitation to relationship, I specifically asked folks to come back to coffee hour and introduce themselves to one new person. Mary, it worked! A woman (a previous longtime parishioner who has started attending again after a decades-long absence) actually came to coffee hour and she met someone new! The person she met ended up coming to a newcomer's class that same day. Just one little effort had visible, tangible payoff."

An old Chinese proverb goes like this: *When you hear something, you will forget it. When you see something, you will remember it. But not until you do something will you understand it.* By taking the suggestion to intentionally focus on what he could do as an individual rather than tackle the bigger issue of changing the entire parish's culture, this priest experienced firsthand how Invite Welcome Connect can bring about change, one person at a time.

RELATIONAL: Critical to the work of Invite Welcome Connect is the core value of relational ministry. The way to effectively close the back door of our churches and empower folks for ministry is to be in relationship with them! Archbishop Desmond Tutu has a beautiful saying that speaks to this: "We say in our African idiom, 'A person is a person through other persons.' The solitary human being is a contradiction in terms. I need you in order to be me as you need me in order to be you. We are caught up in a delicate network of interconnectedness. I have gifts that you don't, and you have gifts I don't—voila! We are made different so that we may know our need of one another. The completely self-sufficient human being is subhuman. Thus diversity, difference, is of the essence of who we are. A rainbow is a rainbow only and precisely because it is made up of different colors. We are placed on earth to discover that we are made for togetherness, for interdependence, for complementarity."

> Diversity, difference, is of the essence of who we are. A rainbow is a rainbow only and precisely because it is made up of different colors.
>
> — Desmond Tutu

Ultimately, Invite Welcome Connect is all about relationship. We have been created and we exist in the image of a relational God, and our spiritual and human connections are what give our lives meaning. Neuroscience research confirms that we humans are hardwired for connection; our nervous systems actually want us to connect with other human beings. So it should not surprise us that when people join our churches but do not find relationships or connections that are so vital to their spiritual, mental, and emotional well-being, they go right out the back door in search of this deep longing! People have a profound yearning for community, and our churches can fulfill this longing by becoming safe havens of loving-kindness.

ACCOUNTABLE: In the early stages of determining the vision and core values of Invite Welcome Connect, Bishop Claude E. Payne and I had a conversation about working with the newcomer pilot congregations, and he asked me this, "So you are holding these congregations accountable to following through with your created assessments?" His question inspired me to define the fourth core value for this ministry! We are accountable: first to God and the gospel, then to each other and those in our communities of faith.

I first heard Mary Parmer speak at a church conference several years ago. As a result, we invited Mary to come to our parish, Messiah Episcopal Church in Rhinebeck, New York, to lead us in a weekend of reflection on how to welcome newcomers. It was a game-changing moment for us, and we felt as a congregation like I had the first time I heard Mary speak: This ministry of welcome was true and profound. And doable.

What I heard Mary say was at the core of why I became a parish priest. Over the years since my ordination, I had become distracted by any number of presentations on church growth that relied on gimmicks, clichés, and fear. Instead, Mary focused on listening to the stories of the people in our congregation and a willingness to listen to the stories of newcomers. The ministry of Invite Welcome Connect relies on the belief that we listen to our stories and we honor them. The call to a ministry of listening was why I had become a priest, but along the way I had lost that focus. Mary's words cut straight to the heart of my calling and what I knew to be true.

What makes it true is that this process of welcoming the newcomer has a powerful foundation in the Bible. We are asked to be the bearers of the story of God's love and presence revealed through the men and women of scripture. As Christians, we carry the story of Jesus as an invitation to a new life. Invite Welcome Connect builds on this invitation, making incarnate the truth of our Savior and the challenge inherent in the ubiquitous signs, "The Episcopal Church Welcomes You."

Invite Welcome Connect has given us tools to reconnect with what we all knew to be true. Unintentionally and unconsciously, we had closed ourselves off. We wanted to welcome the stranger and we had great interest and energy for doing so, but we had lost our way. Mary opened our minds and hearts to a new way of being ministers of hospitality and welcome. The truth had always been there in front of us; we just needed to be reminded why we are church and why church matters. Mary did that for me and she did that for our congregation as the fire of the gospel caught us and changed our lives forever.

Richard McKeon
Rector
Episcopal Church of the Messiah
Rhinebeck, New York

STORYTELLING: While the four core values of Invite Welcome Connect are prayerful, intentional, relational, and accountable, the vital element and holy habit of storytelling guides this work. For as long as we have had the capacity of speech, people have been telling stories to make sense of their lives, to make sense of the world. Everyone has a story. Our mission with

Invite Welcome Connect is to ensure we take the time to listen to these stories, not only of the newcomers to our churches but also the stories of long-time members who may have never had the opportunity to share them.

The heart of relational evangelism is sharing our faith journey. Telling our stories opens us up to others with vulnerability and authenticity, and it offers the gift of deep and holy listening while others share their stories. Stories bind us one to another, and our relationship with the Living Word of God is rooted in story, from the first words of creation through the parables told by Jesus and the tales of the apostles traveling to the ends of the earth, telling all the Good News of the risen Christ.

PRAYER

Dear Gracious Lord, we pray this day with holy intention to live into our Baptismal Covenant, to become reflections of Christ in everything we do. We ask you, Lord, for the grace to see others as Jesus sees them, with love and compassion and forgiveness. Give us the courage to implement Invite Welcome Connect in our congregation and open our hearts and minds to holy listening and loving souls so we may take the challenge of creativity seriously and serve you faithfully. *Amen.*

QUESTIONS FOR INDIVIDUALS

1. What are your hopes and dreams for your personal journey of faith?

2. What are your personal hopes and dreams for your congregation?

3. Are you willing to step out of your comfort zone into a place of creativity and possibility? What are some concrete ways you can do this?

QUESTIONS FOR GROUPS

1. Stepping back and looking at your church through the lens of Invite Welcome Connect is not easy. Do you perceive a genuine opportunity and willingness to do this?

2. Transformation happens in our lives when we are able to see old things in new ways, full of new possibilities. What are some of the transformational possibilities you can imagine for your congregation?

Chapter 2

INVITE

Go therefore and make disciples of all nations, baptizing them in the name of the Father and of the Son and of the Holy Spirit, and teaching them to obey everything that I have commanded you. And remember, I am with you always, to the end of the age.
Matthew 28:19-20

Will you proclaim by word and example the Good News of God in Christ?
The Book of Common Prayer

Proclaiming by word and example the good news of God in Christ is an excellent definition of evangelism, and Episcopalians answer this question in the Baptismal Covenant with a resounding, "I will, with God's help!" So why then do we find it so difficult to say the word evangelism, much less talk about our faith or invite someone to church?

Invite: What Jesus Says

"Hey, hon," my wife says from across the room, "did you see we got an invitation in the mail today?"

How can I not drop everything I'm doing and ask: "To what?!?"

Don't the very words "You are invited" bring a sense of excitement and curiosity to us?

So much of *The Book of Common Prayer* liturgy includes a series of invitations. For example, hear someone say, "the Lord be with you" and try not reflexively thinking or saying, "and also with you." The invitation begs for—it invites—but does not compel a response.

Invite Welcome Connect has three parts. Obviously, they are related. But as we've put the practices into place in our congregation, I have come to think they're also primal and progressive: moving from welcome, to connection, to invitation.

As Mary Parmer and others point out in this book, there is something primal, some deep part of our hearts and souls, that craves connection. In an age of increased isolation and political polarity, we especially yearn for places where we can form authentic connections with others. Unless we make those connections, we remain isolated, cut off: the eye that effectively says to the hand, "I have no need of you." Unless we are connected and abide in the source of the fruits of the Spirit, we become self-sustaining, which is unsustainable.

There's also something primal about our desire to be welcomed; our need to be accepted and wanted is met, at least in part, when other people welcome us, whether into a high school group of friends, a college club, or our spouse's family. (In fact, when I'm doing wedding rehearsals, I make a point to tell the parents of both the bride and the groom that there may be no more important point in the whole wedding weekend than when the parents of the newly married couple, perhaps in a toast, say the words, "Welcome to the family.") Whether in a church or a family, unless we feel authentically welcomed, we remain outsiders, no matter how long we participate in the institution.

We are aware of these deeply human needs to be connected and welcomed. But for some reason, we don't give enough attention to our every-bit-as-real need to be invited and to invite. I think part of the reason is that our desire to be invited and the yearning to invite others, while still primal, is higher up on sociologist Abraham Maslow's hierarchy of needs than our needs for connection and welcome. Perhaps that's part of the reason that Jesus, who always wants to move us from a limited, survival mentality to an expansive mentality of abundance, spends so much time inviting others and accepting invitations.

In the Gospel of Matthew, is "follow me, and I will make you fish for people" a command? Or is it an invitation to leave the supposed safety and security of what those fishermen know and discover what Jesus promises?

And how about when Jesus tells Martha in Luke 10:41-42, "you are worried and distracted by many things; there is need of only one thing. Mary has chosen the better part." This is so like Jesus to issue an invitation in the form of an observation. Jesus invites Martha— and the "Martha" tendency in all of us—to move beyond being so focused on providing needs that we miss receiving blessings.

God knows this about us: As we move our way up from "I'm surviving" to "I'm thriving," we feel more secure and become more outwardly focused.

As we become more outwardly focused, we get in touch with our primal need to be invited to something: We feel safe enough to want to be invited beyond what we already know and have mastered. We yearn to be invited to places we have not seen and to meet people we have not met. We want to be invited to experience things that are new. And as we progress in our spiritual development and an abundant, expansive mentality starts to feel more and more natural, we instinctively want to invite others into this nurturing environment.

If you are excited about a new restaurant you've discovered, no one has to tell you to invite others there. It's second nature to share excitement. The task of churches who want a ministry of invitation to organically and authentically grow is to take the ministries of connection and welcome so seriously that those who are there progress from scarcity to expansiveness—and we can't help but invite others into what we have discovered.

John Ohmer
Rector, The Falls Church Episcopal
Falls Church, Virginia

The primary objective of the Invite essential is to help Episcopalians overcome this reticence about evangelism. The Invite principle is about inviting people not only into a relationship with you and others in your congregation but also inviting them into a relationship with God through Jesus. We often hear people say they don't need to go to church to be Christian. As Episcopalians, we proclaim each week our belief in the importance of coming together as people of faith to learn, pray, question, and explore. We believe that a relationship with Christ is strengthened by involvement in a faith community.

This is why Invite is so important. Many people are waiting for — hungry for — an invitation, to be a part of a community of faith. Inviting someone to church through a personal invitation is the most effective and essential act of reaching out.

> Evangelism is sharing the faith that is in you and listening and learning from the faith that's in somebody else. It's not just about you talking—it's about listening and sharing; it's about a relationship where God can get in the midst
>
> - Michael B. Curry

Presiding Bishop Michael B. Curry defined evangelism in his concluding remarks in his sermon at the 2015 Invite Welcome Connect Summit: "Evangelism is not what other people say that it is. Evangelism is sharing the faith that is in you and listening and learning from the faith that's in somebody else. It's not just about you talking — it's about listening and sharing; it's about a relationship where God can get in the midst."

Our first order of business must be to create a culture of evangelism in our churches. In *Transforming Evangelism*, author David Gortner writes, "Evangelism is not a programmatic effort… It is a willful, joyful, spiritual discipline of seeing and naming the Holy Spirit at work in ourselves and those we encounter—giving voice to our own grace-filled experiences, and helping others find their voice." David's book is an excellent resource for helping Episcopalians reclaim evangelism as a spiritual practice and discipline, offering an array of compelling discussion questions for individuals and small groups.

In real estate, it's all about "location, location, location." In the church, it is about "invitation, invitation, invitation!" At Church of the Good Shepherd in Dallas, Texas, we thought of ourselves as a warm and friendly place and maybe we were. However, the team we sent to an Invite Welcome Connect conference learned that being inviting involved more than a non-critical, unchallenging self-assessment. Rather, it is important to see ourselves as we truly are, understand how others experience us, and then learn how to invite people into community.

Invitation is intentional, important, planned work. Invitation is best preceded by prayer. Invitation is a simple appeal, offer, or call to another person to join you in an activity and experience you value highly. Invitation is not coercive. Invitation, much like the love of God, offers itself instead of making demands. Invitation puts no pressure on the inviter or the invitee. Invitation is not intimidating when the results are left in God's hands. And excitement and joy can be found in the process of inviting.

At Good Shepherd, we moved from a haphazard series of attempts to follow up and include visitors to a system designed to identify people, not just the first time they visit but just as importantly when they return the second time. And once we know who they are and how to contact them, every guest receives a thank you note from the clergy and three invitations: one to a Christian formation class or Bible study, one to an outreach ministry activity, and one to a fellowship group.

Over the past few years, the Invite essential has increased the strength of the front door of our church as people new to Good Shepherd are introduced to members and other visitors, ministries, and opportunities immediately as they enter. By inviting, welcoming, and connecting new people to the community of Good Shepherd, we have seen good, steady growth that bucks the trend of mainline churches in general, and the Episcopal Church specifically. In 2014, we added fifty-three new members and increased our membership by 5 percent. In 2015, we added 101 new members and increased our membership by almost 10 percent. And in 2016, we again welcomed almost 100 new members, including thirty baptisms and thirty-two confirmations.

We are a neighborhood parish that still values knowing who is here and who is not from Sunday to Sunday. We like to think of ourselves as the "biggest, best small church in Texas." We do not think that we are special or that we learned some unfathomable secret. Rather, we are amazed to be witnesses to the power of God's love enfleshed through Invite. And we are grateful to the growth God has brought.

Thomas S. Hotchkiss
Vicar, Good Shepherd Church & School
Dallas, Texas

Christian author and theologian C.S. Lewis put it this way in his classic on Christian apologetics, *Mere Christianity*: "The Church exists for nothing else but to draw men into Christ, to make them little Christs. If they are not doing that, all the cathedrals, clergy, missions, sermons, even the Bible itself, are simply a waste of time. God became Man for no other purpose. It is even doubtful, you know, whether the whole universe was created for any other purpose."

Recognizing and naming the work of the Holy Spirit in our lives, helping others find their voice, and forming people to be little Jesus Christs in the world, though not the easiest nor the most natural move on our part, requires a combination of our effort and inscrutable divine grace. Establishing an ethos of evangelism starts with clergy, staff, and lay leaders. They should be modeling the practices of Invite. This includes not only preaching and talking about evangelism but also actually doing it, inviting people to worship and to become a part of the church community. Our leaders must show the way, leading by example the practice of invitation.

Episcopal priest Samuel Shoemaker, known for his contributions and service to Alcoholics Anonymous, spoke to the critical issue of clergy leadership in evangelism in an article published January 23, 1949, in *The Living Church*.

> *We must train our lay people in evangelism. This obviously cannot be done unless we are doing it ourselves. We shall fight the air, talk negative nonsense about the wrong kinds of evangelism without ever telling them how to do the right kind. The leaven in a group like that is always somebody who is doing it. The death of a training-*

group is ideas unrelated to people, preachments apart from illustrations, a great deal of "ought" plus a very little "is."

We Episcopalians are noted for our reticence, and we think it one of our virtues; if so, it is a virtue of which we need to repent, for it is not humility, it is pure pride, when we cannot and will not learn how to articulate in a natural, human, arresting, convincing way about why the experience of Christ is meaningful to us. We did not cause this, we are simply beneficiaries; what we have done is nothing to crow about, but what he has done for us is our version of the good news. The big objective "mighty acts" will be remote and theological for many till they get incarnated in modern people whose lives show the effects of the "mighty acts."

We do not want talkers who are not doers, nor preachers who are not experiencers; but we do want our churches filled with laypeople who can make Christ live for other people by showing them how he has met their needs and begun to solve their problems. What we are actually doing with some of our lay people who need and long to do vital spiritual work but whom we continue to use in merely a little mechanical "church-work," is to impact their frustrations, to baptize their conventionality, to endorse their spiritual ineffectiveness, and to make of them spiritual dead-ends and terminals when we should be spiritual fountains and junctions.

This is the aim of Invite Welcome Connect as a ministry of the church, and it points to the deep truth of the Invite practice:

courage. Becoming unafraid of who we are in Christ is an essential practice of discipleship. As Cistercian abbot Thomas Keating suggests, it is a movement away from the "little I" of our egos and toward the great "I AM," the one in whom "all things hold together" (Colossians 1:17). God holds our stories, our faith journeys, and bids us to share them with each other. We become spiritual "junctions" for each other. Our vulnerability bears some particular magic. Beyond the original jitters that attend inviting, it can be an ultimately exhilarating practice.

But we would be remiss if we said this essential of Invite was easy to put into practice. Miguel Escobar, a lay leader and director of Anglican studies at Episcopal Divinity School, wrote about his own challenges with invitation in a blog for "Vital Practices," a ministry of the Episcopal Church Foundation.

> *Whenever I hear about how hard it is to evangelize in the Episcopal Church, I immediately think about five of my closest friends. These five friends are wonderful people. They're thoughtful, socially engaged young adults who balance their commitments to serious issues with a serious sense of fun. And while none of these five currently attend a church, I believe all are open to spiritual/religious exploration. To my mind, anyway, this makes them prime candidates for the Episcopal Church. Because of this, time and time again I have tried to work up the nerve to extend an invitation. And on all but one occasion, I've failed. My reasons for not extending an invitation are plentiful and familiar: I'm worried about what my friends will think of me; I'm concerned over whether the sermon will be good and whether the music will be well chosen; I wonder how I'd feel if, at the end of the day, they aren't interested.*

(An Invite Welcome Connect video) helps to correct all that…When I watched it, I realized how my reasons for not extending the invitation were largely about control and mainly about me. In contrast, this video shows how the initial invitation was just a spark for a much larger transformation. It shows how one person's journey began when a friend invited her to an Episcopal church, but how God and the Holy Spirit took over from there.

Like most people, I need regular reminders that it's not all about me. Evangelism isn't about inviting people to "my" church. There's no way to control what people will think of me, or what will happen during the service that day, or whether my friends are open to starting a new journey. This video highlights the fact that evangelism isn't so much about offering something that's ours to others so much as extending the invitation and getting out of the way. Who have you been meaning to invite to church lately?

Preparing members of our congregations to be evangelists can be accomplished in a variety of creative ways. First and foremost, people need to understand that sharing their faith with actions can be as stirring as sharing their faith with words. As a young child growing up in Mississippi, I will never forget the impact a friend's mother had on me when I saw her pause, make the sign of the cross, and pray whenever she heard an ambulance or fire siren. Her piety made an impression on me in a way that was subtle yet powerful. I've heard many similar stories about the power of faith in action as I take the ministry of Invite Welcome Connect around the country.

In Ohio, a world-renowned heart surgeon looks for "faith flags" in his patients and their families—signs that they are people of faith—and then he boldly asks permission to pray with the patient moments before surgery. While sitting in church one Sunday, a woman in southern Louisiana received the inspiration to donate one of her kidneys to a perfect stranger, and she realizes now that every time she shares that story, she is evangelizing. These folks are sharing their faith in visible, concrete ways. We might ask ourselves, how can we follow this example?

I grew up in a nomadic family that moved about every two years. The pattern continued when I became a military officer. At some point in adolescence my very Italian, very Roman Catholic grandmother gave me a Saint Christopher's medal—even though I was a Methodist at the time. Saint Christopher is the patron saint of travelers, and I wore that medal across America, the Middle East, Europe, and Asia. Even as I drifted away from the church in my mid-twenties, I held fast to my Saint Christopher's medal.

Upon leaving the military, I moved back to Tennessee and helped run a small business with my brother-in-law. Sundays were still more about football than Jesus, but in my late twenties, I began to notice a certain magnetism to the religious world. I had no desire to attend the churches of my youth, but I wanted to give church another try; I just didn't know where.

One night I was playing in a basketball league with some other young professionals, and Dan fouled me hard. He was a decent fellow, so he came over to give me a hand. He noticed my Saint Christopher's medal and told me that he went to a church called St. Christopher's. He said he thought I'd enjoy the worship, the priest gave great sermons, and the people who attended were pretty chill but engaged in the community. Services started at 10 a.m., and I was more than welcome to sit with him if I ever wanted to visit. And then we kept playing ball.

Two weeks later I had the time and the itch to go to church. Not having any other invitations, I decided to give Dan's church a try. He was right; I loved St. Christopher's! Within a month, I was attending confirmation classes. Within six months, I was running the church's Salvation Army kitchen team, and within a year I was on a rector search committee and the head of the acolytes and the youth group. I had never set foot inside an Episcopal church before Dan invited me to St. Christopher's, and today I'm an Episcopal priest.

Take a little chance and invite someone to church. The upside is huge!

Christian Hawley
Associate Rector
St. Matthew's Episcopal Church
Austin, Texas

Of course, sharing our faith with words as well as action is critical, and author and theologian Frederick Buechner writes of the importance of sharing our personal stories in his memoir *Telling Secrets*: "My story is important not because it is mine, God knows, but because if I tell it anything like right, the chances are you will recognize that in many ways it is also yours…it is through our stories that God makes himself known to each of us most powerfully and personally. If this is true, it means that to lose track of our stories is to be profoundly impoverished not only humanly but also spiritually."

One of the resources for learning how to share our faith stories is through a Sharing Faith Dinners idea created by Carol Barnwell of the Diocese of Texas. Designed for eight to twelve people to gather around a meal and share their faith through engaging questions, the dinners provide a welcoming and safe way to articulate faith and build relationships. This concept has been implemented in numerous congregations throughout the Episcopal Church and has been quite an effective way for folks to learn to share their faith in non-threatening environments.

The Invite essential offers a number of tools for helping folks invite others to church, ranging from business cards to car decals. Creating numerous avenues of invitation to invite and involve the local community is another element of this essential. Sometimes it's easier to invite someone to a special event at the church rather than to a worship service. St. Francis Episcopal Church in Houston hosted an arts festival for many years, but until they engaged in Invite Welcome Connect, they never considered giving the festival attendees information about St. Francis or the Episcopal Church. Now the arts festival is seen as an opportunity for invitation. In addition to changes with the festival, St. Francis has implemented several of the Invite practices. In the first year after implementing the Invite Welcome Connect ministry, St. Francis added 142 new members and has continued in steady growth for years. I encourage you to include information about your church with any activity held at your facility; otherwise you are simply a venue. As you open your

> It is through our stories that God makes himself known to each of us most powerfully and personally.
>
> – Frederick Buechner

doors for art shows, community festivals, concerts, blessings of the animals, farmer's markets, etc., ask the question, "Why are we doing this? Does it align with our mission? How is this an opportunity for invitation?"

It was Ash Wednesday 2014, and I was standing in the Holy Comforter parking lot wearing my cassock with a bowl of ashes in my hand. Suddenly a little black Mini Cooper zipped in and nearly ran me over. The driver cracked open her window, peered up at me, and asked, "Is this for real?"

Drive-Thru Ashes at Holy Comforter has been the single-highest generator of growth for our church for the past five years. More people have joined Holy Comforter because of an invitation to worship they received during Drive-Thru Ashes than people who have joined because of visiting on Christmas Eve or Easter. Every Ash Wednesday since 2013, more than 300 people have pulled into our parking lot to receive ashes. These brief moments provide an opportunity to pray, provide pastoral care, and importantly, invite them to church on Sunday.

The name of the woman who almost ran me over in 2014 is Linda. She received ashes that morning, and later in the day emailed the church office, writing that this was the first time any church had made her think about the love of Christ in the middle of the week. Linda was with us for worship the next Sunday and, as she puts it, her life was transformed. She reaffirmed her baptismal vows when the bishop visited later that year, she committed herself to Bible study and daily prayer, and eventually she even led our capital campaign to build a new church.

Drive-Thru Ashes has become an opportunity to invite people to church on Sunday, and since we started in 2013, Holy Comforter has doubled in size. But there is more to it than the numbers. Linda met Jesus and experienced a transformation on that day. By opening our hearts and inviting others, our church has also undergone a transformation in our journey to know Jesus.

Jimmy Abbott
Rector, Holy Comforter Episcopal Church
Spring, Texas

Within the Invite essential, it is important to consider not only how well you know your church's neighbors but also how well they know you. Are you partnering with other community groups to effect change in your community? Are the clergy, staff, and lay leaders committed to civic involvement? Even after I closed my business and joined the staff at St. Stephen's, I continued my membership in the Beaumont Rotary Club. This turned out to be an excellent decision: My relationships with business leaders in Beaumont were instrumental in the creation of many of our community-wide ministries.

Examining communication as an evangelism tool is another vital component of Invite. This includes not only how we communicate internally with those already in our congregations but also with those in our communities and beyond. What story does your newsletter tell about you? Are you telling the tale of a flagging, depressed congregation desperate for money and volunteers? Or is the church committed to being a mighty presence, despite its size? What welcome mat does your church extend on its website and through its social media presence? These are the new front doors to your church. Do people see energy, vitality, and transformation in your online community or are you still promoting Easter Sunday services in October?

Social media in particular is a gift to the Invite principle. If you struggle with the face-to-face invitation, a simple Facebook, Twitter, or Instagram invitation is easy to extend. Social media also allows for a broader reach and can be a strategic tool for evangelism. Trinity Episcopal Church in The Woodlands, Texas, had a Facebook page but initially used it primarily for in-house announcements. After they began implementing Invite Welcome Connect in their congregation, they experimented with using Facebook for advertising. Spending $127.62, the church's "Blessings of the Backpacks and Teachers" Sunday service appeared in front of a targeted audience of up to 10,000 Facebook users per day. Seventy-one users clicked on their ad, which took them to the church's website and event page. Trinity's website experienced a 17 percent increase in first-time visits, and attendance at the Sunday worship exceeded 600, with many new first-time visitors.

I assure clergy and lay leaders who attend Invite Welcome Connect presentations that it isn't necessary they participate in social media on an individual basis. But I urge them to consider how to use social media in effective and meaningful ways, leveraging it as a creative tool for evangelism on behalf of their congregations. I could fill this book with stories of how the use of social media has impacted both individuals and congregations in a positive, life-giving light. You probably have your own stories of personal experiences with social media (both good and bad).

Social media is a tool that requires intentional and wise oversight, but I strongly encourage congregations to harness the power of social media and up-to-date websites as a vital part of the ministry of Invite Welcome Connect.

Michelle Shih, director of digital editions and lifestyle for *O* magazine, articulates this challenge for those who might be reluctant to engage in any social media endeavors. "You might think social media isn't for you. Here's why you're wrong... You owe it to yourself to remain relevant. You don't want to fall out of touch because you've decided that what is current no longer belongs to you. Social media won't make you young. But letting the world leave you behind is what makes you old."

> Social media won't make you young. But letting the world leave you behind is what makes you old.
>
> – Michelle Shih

It had been three years. We had three years of meetings, conversations, starts, stops, sprints, and a bit of confusion. Communication was strong, but when members of the New Member Ministry Team finally had a plan, something would happen, and the plan would be delayed. I will forever remember the moment when I knew the tides had turned and the leaders were ready to lead. It began with a sign showing where to park—where to turn. For almost seven years, our worshiping community had placed signs on the road to help others know where to turn. The signs evolved over time, but the message remained the same: "Holy Spirit Parking."

In a meeting, one of the members of the Invite Team asked, "Can't we change our signs, so they do something more than just point to the parking?" He went on to say, "The church next to us has these great welcoming

signs that say things like, 'You have arrived.' Our signs say, 'Holy Spirit Parking.'" I asked him what he thought our signs should say. He said, "I don't know. How about something about Invite Welcome Connect?" Immediately, we got to work on the phrasing and the look of these new signs. A conversation about helping people know where to turn became a turning point in the life of our New Member Ministry. This momentum became contagious, and the Welcome and Connect teams each followed suit and stepped up their game. It took three years to get here but we finally all turned together!

Jason T. Roberts

Rector

Episcopal Church of the Holy Spirit

San Antonio, Texas

The deep truth of Invite is courage. It takes courage to invite someone to church. It requires a willingness to set aside fear and to take a chance. But as Miguel Escobar says, "Evangelism isn't so much about offering something that's ours to others so much as extending the invitation and getting out of the way." We need to invite, and then leave the rest up to God and the Holy Spirit. As Saint Paul writes in 2 Timothy 1:7, "For God hath not given us a spirit of fear but of power, and of love, and of a sound mind" (KJV). The Holy Spirit, powerful and lovely, is always at work in our inviting. The immediate effect may be veiled, at least temporarily, to us; we may not know how, when, or if the person will respond. But that is God's work, not ours. We are simply called to summon the courage to Invite.

PRAYER

Gracious God, who has given us not a spirit of fear, but the power of love, grant us courage to step out of our comfort zones, to invite someone to church, to see and welcome the Other, and to be willing to discern the gifts God has placed within us. Help us claim our life's work as ministry, as holy sacred work. Open our hearts and minds with holy listening and loving souls and give us the moral courage to think outside the box, to imagine the possibilities for this congregation, a beloved community of the Jesus Movement. *Amen.*

QUESTIONS FOR INDIVIDUALS

1. Have you ever been invited to church? How did that feel? How did you respond?

2. Have you ever invited someone to church? If so, reflect on that experience. If you haven't invited someone to church, what has stopped you from doing so?

3. Think about your story of faith. Why are you a Christian? Write 4-5 thoughts about why you follow Christ. Then think about your church. Why do you attend church in that particular place? What is compelling to you? What feeds you?

4. Courage is presented as the core truth of the Invite principle. Do you agree? What other traits and values are important for this aspect of the Invite Welcome Connect ministry?

5. Think about your congregation and its activities. Which ones lend themselves to invitations for guests? If you were to invite someone to your worship service, what would you worry about? What would you be most excited to share with newcomers?

QUESTIONS FOR GROUPS

1. Do your clergy, staff, and lay leaders teach, preach, and model Invite (personal invitation and evangelism)? In what ways? What ideas do you have for expanding this Invite component?

2. What are you doing in an organized way to invite new people to visit your church?

3. Do you provide any physical tools to your members to help them invite others? What are they? What else might you offer?

4. How do you prepare your congregation to be evangelists? Do you offer education/training/guides for sharing their faith journey/stories?

5. What are the creative avenues your church offers to invite the local community to visit? Do you intentionally connect these activities with information about your church?

6. How well do you know (and how much are you involved with) the community surrounding your church?

7. What is your church/clergy/staff relationship with local civic/community groups? What could be expanded or improved?

8. What does your congregation offer in the way of communication, both outside and in-house? Have you cultivated a relationship with your local media outlets? How could you do so?

9. Is your website up-to-date, relevant, and newcomer and mobile friendly? Are you using social media as an evangelism tool? How could you expand or improve your web and social media presence?

RESOURCES: The appendix includes a checklist for the Invite essential as well as some tools for implementation. For more ideas and resources, visit: www.invitewelcomeconnect. sewanee.edu

Chapter 3

WELCOME

Welcome one another, therefore, just as Christ has welcomed you, for the glory of God.
                    Romans 15:7

If we are to love our neighbors, before doing anything else we must see our neighbors. With our imagination as well as our eyes, that is to say like artists, we must see not just their faces but the life behind and within their faces. Here it is love that is the frame we see them in.
            Frederick Buechner, *Beyond Words*

Welcome is the ministry of hospitality, and this essential covers everything from first impressions to follow-up with visitors. Welcome asks the question, "Do your clergy, staff, and lay leaders teach, preach, and model a theology of welcome and hospitality?" Most church leaders believe their churches are friendly, but Welcome extends beyond being nice (and honestly, some congregations have a way to go before reaching the friendly threshold, much less embracing the Welcome essential).

In her book, *The Rule of Benedict: Insight for the Ages,* Joan Chittister paraphrases the ancient writings of the rabbis, "Hospitality is one form of worship. Come right in and disturb our perfect lives—you are the Christ for us today." Welcoming the stranger is welcoming Jesus. Jesus pays attention to what is going on around him and especially to those people he encounters on a daily basis. He models for us a new way of seeing the other—a way of love, compassion, and forgiveness. The gospels are full of stories about Jesus being fully present with the people he meets. In his study of how Jesus loves, Paul Miller writes in his book, *Love Walked Among Us,* that the gospels mention Jesus looking at people about forty times. Jesus' compassion for people is often preceded by his looking at them. In the Gospel of Luke, Jesus sees the widow at Nain, looking into her eyes and heart, and he has compassion for her and raises her son from the dead. Luke's Gospel also tells of Jesus entering Jericho and encountering Zacchaeus, the chief tax collector. Jesus *sees* Zacchaeus up in the sycamore tree and invites himself to Zacchaeus's house. He *sees* the Samaritan woman at the well in the Gospel of John, and his interaction with her transforms her life.

The etymology of the New Testament word hospitality is *philoxenia: philo* is derived from the ancient Greek words *philia* (φιλία) and *xenia* (ξενία), meaning literally a love of strangers. Considered a gospel directive, hospitality is mentioned in Acts 28:7, Romans 12:13, 1 Timothy 3:2; 5:10, Titus 1:8, Hebrews 13:2, and 1 Peter 4:9, giving Christians ample proof that we are called to this ministry.

Welcome: What Jesus Says

A Samaritan woman came to draw water, and Jesus said to her,
"Give me a drink."

John 4:7

The story was never supposed to go this way. A Jewish man walks to the well at midday and encounters a Samaritan woman. She has a bucket; he does not but that doesn't matter. He should walk away before he is polluted by contact or someone sees them together.

The story was never supposed to go this way, but you can't tell that to Jesus. Instead, when he sees this sister alone at the well, he draws near. Though he is the true source of living water, he asks *her* for a drink. Though he is the fulfillment of all the law and the prophets, she has to remind him of the rules…and then he breaks them to linger and talk with her.

What kind of Lord of lords is this? Jesus doesn't assume he knows everything. Instead, he opens the way for conversation, listens to her questions, honors her answers, and appears genuinely prepared to be changed by her wisdom.

Although his disciples say nothing when they come upon the scandalous scene, it's not difficult to read their minds: *Not again, Jesus! Why do you keep doing this?* Perhaps Jesus knows the payoff will be worth violating these societal codes. By John 4:28, the Samaritan woman is running back to the village as the first apostle to tell the world about the new life she has found in Jesus Christ.

For me, this story is the ultimate in good news and the pattern for any ministry of welcome and hospitality. Where others heap on scorn, Jesus has compassion. When others run away, Jesus moves closer. Where others assume they've got it all figured out, Jesus is curious. And perhaps most striking: where others might see someone less wise or even less human—someone with nothing but need—Jesus sees the possibility of blessing. His wide-open arms and spirit change the narrative. They change everything.

This may very well be the deep truth of Welcome: When we open ourselves to receive those who have been defined as "other" because of race or class or ideology or neighborhood or culture or gender or sexual orientation or physical ability or any host of hierarchies, when we approach the "other" with compassion, courage, curiosity, and anticipation of blessing, the world (and we) can be made new.

Imagine if churches truly nourished those capacities in one another. Imagine how compassion, courage, curiosity, and receptivity to blessing could play out in our ministries. For instance, consider the old man at the soup kitchen, the one who has been coming for years. Maybe he has something to teach the church. Maybe he knows more about serving food and running a kitchen than the volunteers currently staffing it. We will only know if we become more like Jesus at the well. Honor your brother enough to draw near, let curiosity lead, and expect a blessing. It will come.

I think of women I've known at domestic violence shelters and the wisdom several of them could preach about strength and resilience. I think of youth who want nothing to do with church, and yet they have taught me a great deal about what it means to be in authentic relationships. I think of so many who are on the margins of my life, so many who could actually bless and teach me if I set aside prejudice, show up, be curious, and let God work in the space between us.

Life would probably be easier if welcome was simply opening the doors and saying, "You're welcome to what we've got, and what we've got is the best!" Authentic welcome comes from a more humble place. I don't know what you need or what you love or what you bring. I'm not sure what I have is the "best." No, I welcome because I long to cross this dividing wall and enter into relationship with you. I welcome because my life is incomplete without the flecks of light and wisdom God will only reveal through you, your presence, and your story. I welcome because Jesus welcomed first.

Stephanie Spellers
Canon for Evangelism, Reconciliation,
and Creation Care
The Episcopal Church

Given these gospel imperatives, I recall one of my early journal entries, which pondered the ubiquitous "The Episcopal Church Welcomes You" signs.

The Episcopal Church welcomes you…is it risky business? I ponder this as I am tediously peeling off the old Episcopal Church sticker on my car's rear window so I can attach my new one.

I am working on this newcomer project and getting ready to head out of town to visit one of our churches in the Diocese of Texas when a young woman walks up and asks if she may use my restroom. Immediately my mind races: Do I let her in my home? Can I trust this perfect stranger? What if…And then in the middle of these thoughts, I remember the sermon I preached two weeks ago when I said that "seeing as God sees…and loving as God loves…. is risky business." So, I take the risk and invite her into the house. I learn that she is a foreign exchange student from Latvia, living in the United States for the summer, selling books door to door. After she comes out of the restroom, I hand her a bottle of water, wish her God's blessings, and say goodbye. A small thing, yes. But a gift. A test to see if I will do what I preach and teach. How will I treat this other, this stranger who has shown up on my doorstep? Welcoming her, inviting her in, is indeed risky business, but oh, how gratifying!

I could share a plethora of stories with you from people who have walked through the doors of churches all over the country and left feeling as if they have been neither seen nor acknowledged. My journal entry from eight years ago (prior to beginning the newcomer ministry project) tells of my firsthand visitor experience at a church north of Austin, Texas. After presenting a workshop at a diocesan wardens and vestry conference, the vestry of this church invited me to help them discern whether or not they should hire a newcomer coordinator, so I decided to visit the church as a mystery guest. My journal recounts the experience:

> *I ease out of my driveway at 9:30 a.m. on this overcast, drizzly Sunday morning, and at exactly 10 a.m., I pull into the parking lot of the church. Given that it is the Sunday after Easter and generally a light attendance day, the number of cars already there surprises me. At exactly 10:05 a.m., I walk behind a red-haired woman into the narthex of the church and stand beside the visitor book, waiting for someone to greet me. No one is there. People are milling around, and a person dressed as a verger walks past me two times. I wait. At 10:15 a.m., I spot the red-haired woman standing near one of the entrances to the nave and motion for her to come over to me. I strike up a conversation with her and find out she is a cradle Episcopalian and has been a member of this church since last November. She decided on this church after looking at eleven church websites (she liked the familiar liturgy in the bulletin that was posted on the site). When I asked her about being a newcomer, she said she went to a coffee for newcomers (which they have once a month) and signed up for a Tuesday night women's Bible study but never attended because she can't drive at night.*

By now, it is 10:25 a.m., and a woman approaches us with a handful of bulletins. I take one and head across the narthex to a side hall where I see three men (one in a clergy collar) come out of a meeting room. The clergy person looks straight at me but does not speak. The second man comes over to me and says, "I don't think I know you…. my name is Ed." It is 10:30 a.m. (time for the service to begin), and Ed is the very first person to approach and welcome me this morning.

The service is beautiful, the choir lovely, and the sermon thought provoking. As I peruse the worship bulletin, I notice the "Welcome Guest" blurb, which reads, "Visitors and guests, please let us know more about you by taking a moment to fill out a Visitor Card and drop it in the Offertory Plate or sign in the guest book found in the Narthex."

I look for the Visitor Card in the slots behind the pew, and this is what I find instead: a half-torn pledge card, a dirty Kleenex, a crinkled-up Easter lily order card, a crinkled-up pledge card, a prayer request card, and a memorial flowers order card. There's no Visitor Card in sight, not in the pews behind me or in front of me. Communion hymns are being sung, and the woman beside me notes my Daughter of the King cross and says under her breath that they have a large chapter here. I whisper, "Where are the Visitor Cards?" And she says, "Oh, I don't think we've had those in the pews in two or three years."

In the early years of developing the newcomer ministry project, two heartbreaking stories came my way. The first was from a young married woman who had moved with her family to Texas shortly after her husband was called up to serve his country in Iraq. Given their prior active membership in an Episcopal church in another town and the desire to get their kids involved in children's ministry, the young mother set out to find a nearby church. Although she did not find her neighborhood Episcopal church very friendly, she joined anyway and immediately attempted to get involved. But she became disheartened. A year later, she still attended worship on Sunday mornings but few, if any, people spoke to her. Although her children liked their Sunday school classes, this young mother, dealing with her introverted nature and her husband's long absence, was unhappy. She told me: "I go to church, and no one sees me."

Another story came with a late-night phone call from a friend who had moved to another southern state. A Texas native and cradle Episcopalian who was very active in her church and diocesan ministries, she nevertheless made the difficult decision to move across the country for a job promotion. So what did this smart, professional, early-50's woman do right after she moved into her new home? She began visiting all the Episcopal churches in her area. As we talked on the phone, my friend lamented, "Mary, in every single church I've attended, it's as if they don't even see me. No one sees me!" She had signed guest registers and written her name on welcome cards for newcomers. The only follow-up she received was a form letter with a pledge card.

When I finally decided to visit an Episcopal church, I had high expectations. I had spent my entire life in a conservative evangelical denomination, but a small amount of seminary education had whetted my appetite for a church with more theological depth. Also, the birth of my daughter had made my wife and I realize we could not raise her in a place that viewed her (consciously or not) as a second-class citizen.

I was looking for something. I was a seeker. Like many evangelicals, I loved reading N.T. Wright and C.S. Lewis, so the Episcopal Church seemed a natural place to look. Because I was a ministry leader with obligations at my current church, I had to go to an Episcopal service that was early enough that I could still make it on time to worship at my church. I found a service at a large parish just a mile from my house. I got up early, put on my church clothes, and set out on my church adventure. I walked in that first morning and the greeter welcomed me, handed me a worship bulletin… and that was it. No one else spoke to me. That was okay; it was the early service, and I was just a young guy among a lot of older people. They probably assumed I was someone's grandson.

I went back again the next week, and after the service I filled out the visitor registration card that was in the pew. I checked the box on the card that indicated I would like to speak to a priest. The silence that week was deafening. No emails, no phone calls, not even a form letter so many churches send to guests. I assumed my card had gotten lost. I went back the next week and was greeted again at the door and handed a bulletin. No one else spoke to me. No one shook my hand at the peace. I filled out the visitor card again and checked the box that indicated my desire to speak to a priest. By Wednesday of that third week, I decided to email the rector of the parish. I worked at a church myself and knew how easy it was for a visitor card to get lost. I went to this congregation's wonderful website and found the rector's email address. I emailed and told him I had visited his parish for the last three Sundays and that I had some questions about the Episcopal Church. I am sad to report that he never responded.

The following Sunday I visited the 7:30 a.m. service at a different parish. Over the course of the following week, I received eight different forms of contact from the parish. The rector, the associate, and the curate each sent me an email. I received an invitation to attend a lunch for recent guests. I received a general letter from the rector, and the director of Christian formation called to invite me to Sunday school and sent me a letter describing all of the adult education offerings. Finally, the curate also called and invited me out to lunch.

I was confirmed in that parish the following spring, and my wife was confirmed a year later. We had some wonderful years at our home parish and after discernment we went to the Seminary of the Southwest in Austin. Today I am a priest, and ironically, I am in charge of training our congregation to implement Invite Welcome Connect at our parish. I often reflect on my very different experiences at those first two parishes I visited. I am so glad that I didn't give up on the Episcopal Church after my first experience. I hope we extend a welcome similar to the one I received at the second church, which became my spiritual home.

Tom Dahlman
Rector, Emmanuel Episcopal Church
Shawnee, Oklahoma

These stories, sadly, are not outliers but common experiences for many church visitors. We can do better. We must do better.

In *An Altar in the World,* author Barbara Brown Taylor addresses "the practice of encountering others." She speaks of the practice of "coming face to face with another human being...preferably someone different enough to qualify as a capital O other....and at least entertaining the possibility that this is one of the faces of God."

Brown Taylor implores us to practice encountering others, especially with those who usually sneak right past us, people who are performing some mundane service such as taking an order or handing us change. She writes: "Here is someone who exists even when she is not ringing up your groceries, as hard as that may be for you to imagine. She is someone's daughter, maybe someone's mother as well. She has a home she returns to when she hangs up her apron here, a kitchen that smells of last night's supper, a bed where she occasionally lies awake at night wrestling with her own demons and angels." Sometimes all that is required is to look as Jesus does, to meet the person's eyes for a moment, to say thanks or engage in conversation. Sometimes this simple act helps people feel like they have been seen, not as a cashier or waitress, teacher, mechanic, or doctor, but as people of value. Brown Taylor says this profound practice almost always is met by inner resistance: We don't want to encounter another person at the cash register. We are in a hurry. We just want our groceries.

The deep truth of Welcome is seeing the other. Jesus invites us to see one another in the way of love, and he models both relational evangelism and holy hospitality for us. We are called to really see every single person with whom we have contact on a daily basis as well as with every single person who walks into the doors of our church. To see with the eyes of God is to see humanity as Christ sees humanity, with unconditional love. In 1 Samuel 16:7, we hear, "For the Lord does not see as mortals see; they look on the outward appearance, but the Lord looks on the heart." We all know how difficult this is but imagine what our churches would be like if they were filled with people who had the ability to really see others, people who have stopped looking through the narrow lens of their own world and are willing to see and acknowledge the other, welcoming them with open arms and hearts into our communities of faith. How would our stories change if we helped people feel authentically welcome, if we were sincerely interested in helping people find genuine connections in our churches, if we offered relationship rather than simply membership?

> For the Lord does not see as mortals see; they look on the outward appearance, but the Lord looks on the heart.
>
> – Samuel 16:7

The friend I spoke of earlier in this chapter, the "Texas native and cradle Episcopalian," finally found a church home a good distance from where she lived, and she later wrote of her experience in *The Texas Episcopalian*, the newspaper of the Diocese of Texas:

> While chatting with a greeter, I was invited by him to the upcoming newcomer dinner simply because, 'It's important to meet people in a new city so you won't be lost." Relationship versus membership. During that dinner the vicar used the same metaphor in describing what every individual should expect in his or her parish life – a relationship. One week later, a six-year-old helped

me write my name tag. Advent found me still visiting. During the peace, as they did with each other, I was also greeted by name. At Christmas, deeply grateful for God's comfort and care during my journey, I dropped a check in the plate. When the church sent a letter blessing my giving for its use in helping the Body of Christ, they tugged at my heart because they told me what was important to theirs…With that blessing I transferred my membership and started a new relationship. How many forms? Just the sign-in at the newcomer dinner. After all, they already knew me.

In the early years of developing this ministry, I ran across a thought-provoking blog post written by Daniel Simon, who was at the time serving as an associate priest at Trinity Wall Street located in lower Manhattan, New York City. The post said this: "Greeters and ushers are God's stand-ins and ambassadors. Because you are standing at the threshold and are the first person people speak to when they enter, you hold a huge amount of spiritual power. Because you are the first person they meet, people will project onto you all the assumptions and expectations they have about God before they walked in that door, positive or negative. How you respond will either challenge or reinforce those assumptions. Your actions of welcoming them may make all the difference in their experience of Trinity, and even of divinity."

Greeters and ushers are God's stand-ins and ambassadors.

– Daniel Simon

At Saint John the Evangelist Episcopal Church in Saint Paul, Minnesota, we have come to find that welcome and connection are on a continuum. For us, the work of welcome flows into the work of connection, and it is very difficult to name the spot where one ends and the other begins. Numerous times we have learned the hard way that just because we welcome someone to our church does not mean they'll stay.

We have also learned that this work is quintessentially relational. This is a hard truth for us in Minnesota. Culturally we are predisposed toward introversion and reserve. While Minnesotans epitomize politeness (think "Minnesota Nice"), there is often a hesitation to move out of our comfort zone, to welcome the stranger, to risk the embarrassment that might come from saying the wrong thing or introducing ourselves to someone who has been a member for fifty years. We have also found that building community means more than implementing systems of tracking or programs of member connection—we can and have done these things—but we also have to slowly change our culture toward one of radical welcome and deep connection. We have discovered that fostering this kind of culture means that the leaders of the church, lay and ordained, need to disciple other members in this work. This might mean being ready to mentor and guide (even for the twentieth time) the shy greeter on how to spot and graciously welcome a visitor. For our vestry, it means each member is involved in the work of greeting and welcome so that the experience is a shared one at our top level of leadership.

As a priest in the parish, I am less worried about people trying to bond with me than with facilitating relationships with other members, making the connection and then gracefully stepping aside to see what grows. My job is also to lift up members who have naturally and authentically exemplified this spirit of welcome and connection.

Recently our parish suffered the loss of Don, a beloved and longtime member. Don had been at Saint John's for several decades and had been involved in just about every ministry. He had been a vestry member and warden, the longest and most regularly serving volunteer in our homeless shelter, an avid participant in both our younger and older men's groups, and a founding member of our clinic in Uganda (to name a few). Yet, when he died, the group I heard from the most, the people who came to express their grief and to work through the loss, were recent members. I heard story after story about the ways in which Don had naturally welcomed them. They told me he had exuded graciousness, inviting visitors to coffee hour, introducing them to friends, bringing new guys to the men's groups, and greeting their children by name. Don had, unbeknownst to me, been our greatest asset in new member welcome and connection. He did it without being a part of any official program, and he had communicated authenticity and a deep interest in the individual in front of him at a given time.

Don did all of this out of the spotlight and unofficially. Part of the work of a discipling church is to know the stories of the saints who have shaped and formed their particular faith community, and then sharing those stories, as a way to teach other members about how we can best practice our faith. In this case, Don has become an example that I can point to in the area of Christian welcome and connection as we work to transform our culture from merely hospitable to radically welcoming, a place of deep and lasting connections in the body of Christ.

Jered Weber-Johnson
Rector, St. John the Evangelist Episcopal Church
St. Paul, Minnesota

While some people can make the Welcome essential seem easy, it is a challenge for many individuals and congregations. In most situations, the Welcome essential does not just happen. There is no magical, snap-your-fingers solution. Along with a culture shift in individual and collective practices of intentionally seeing, acknowledging and welcoming newcomers, an intentional and systematic structure must be in place. This is where implementing the Welcome assessments comes into play.

St. Thomas, like many Episcopal churches, tried for years to offer an opportunity immediately following the final Sunday morning service for people to "meet and greet." Those gatherings were attempted in places that required parishioners and newcomers to travel somewhere in the building, either the parish hall or the courtyard if the weather was nice. The response was underwhelming to say the least, and the reality was that after the obligatory handshake with the clergy, most people were out the door, in their cars, and exiting our parking lot within minutes.

When Mary Parmer came to work with our congregation, we brainstormed about the unique challenges of that component of our Welcome ministry. She suggested we move the gathering to a place that people did not have to travel to and could not avoid—the narthex. More than a few people, myself included, thought both silently and aloud, "The narthex, you can't do it there!" But like so many things with the Invite Welcome Connect ministry, a more appropriate response would have been, "Why not?"

We took Mary's suggestion and set aside those "But we've always done it this way..." thoughts and proceeded. We asked volunteers to provide cookies (homemade or store-bought) and something to drink. Our intention was to create a space that people could not avoid, but in reality, we created something that people now look forward to! Our narthex remains full for quite a while following the service with people who have been coming for years and people who just walked in the door spending time together, sharing more than the obligatory "Hello," or "How are you doing?"

This gathering also provides an opportunity for our designated greeters to gather more information about our visitors as we try to help them move deeper and more fully into the life of our community. I am continually amazed at the way this simple offering has become such a critical component of our Invite Welcome Connect ministry!

Paul Pradat
Rector, St. Thomas Episcopal Church
Huntsville, Alabama

The Welcome essential is not only about seeing the other and improving how we greet and welcome folks; it also requires fresh eyes in examining our facilities, inside and out. What needs to be changed in our physical facilities in order that we are perceived as a welcoming place? This essential asks us to evaluate every facet of our buildings from the sanctuary to hallways, assuring they are spaces that feel welcoming and open to nourishing relationships.

A declining congregation with less than eighty in attendance on Sunday morning, and located in a region with a shrinking population, Good Shepherd Church in Parkersburg, West Virginia, was not in a positive place when we hosted a diocesan evangelism conference led by Mary Parmer in April 2016.

We had added very few new members over the past several years. People avoided being greeters, and evangelism was only a word. Our own members had trouble figuring out which door to use to get to and from the sanctuary. If a visitor wanted to join us for coffee in the parish hall, they had to pass by five doors that led to the parking lot and their cars. Most of them took one of those doors.

After the conference, we realized our facility was fundamentally unwelcoming and confusing. A Welcome team put together plans to commandeer one poorly used room, one poorly located room, and a small bathroom and convert them into a Welcome Center. They presented a $240,000 plan to transform the poorly used space into a Welcome Center and a modern nursery. The plan was presented and executed in about five months. The new Welcome Center opened in November 2017.

And wow, has it ever made a difference! We started putting a sign outside on Sunday that says, "Use this door." Isn't that a radical idea? Now everyone knows how to enter the Welcome Center. Instead of a cramped area to greet parishioners and visitors after church, we have a comfortable space with a sink and dishwasher, a warm and welcoming place where folks naturally gravitate.

Welcome teams were reorganized and retrained, and with the tool of the new Welcome Center, they have enthusiastically taken to their task of welcoming. We have added more than a dozen members in the last year.

People speak of how friendly our church is and how welcome they feel when they come to visit. Our whole attitude toward evangelism has changed. We now know that Episcopalians can do evangelism very well.

Hal Foss
Lay Leader
Memorial Church of the Good Shepherd
Parkersburg, West Virginia

BEFORE. The crowded space had doors to two rooms and a bathroom. The ladder is in the corridor to the sanctuary.

AFTER: This shows the Welcome Center from the same angle as the before photo. The arches in the background are part of the corridor leading to the sanctuary.

For visitors and newcomers, the welcome they receive in our churches may be a lifeline. I know it was for me. When I was weary and wounded, the Episcopal church was a sanctuary of healing. I was truly, deeply welcomed, and for that gift, I am eternally thankful. I have shared some of the horror stories that I have heard from people who felt unwelcome in Episcopal churches. I offer those as cautionary tales, reminders that we have opportunities each and every day to be places of radical hospitality. I have also heard and experienced just as many stories from those who were welcomed with open arms.

We bear witness to God's grace when we intentionally practice the ministry of holy hospitality. Part of our responsibility with Invite Welcome Connect is to remind new folks they are now on the other side of welcome, and it's their job to ensure their particular communities of faith are safe havens of grace, love, and welcome for those who remain on the outside. Becoming conscious and aware of this issue is the first step one can take.

PRAYER

Gracious Lord, we pray this day with holy intention to live into our baptismal covenant to become reflections of Christ in everything we do. We ask you for the grace to see others as Jesus sees them in the way of love and compassion and forgiveness. Let us welcome the stranger with open arms. Help us serve faithfully, taking the challenge of creativity seriously, and opening our hearts and minds with holy listening and loving souls. *Amen.*

A bruised reed he will not break,
and a dimly burning wick he will not quench.
Isaiah 42:3

The church is full of bruised reeds and dimly burning wicks. They are children of God who have been bruised, hurt, rejected, and sometimes left to the side to die. They are bruised because they felt as though they did not fit in. Sadly, some have been told in no uncertain terms that they were not welcome. Perhaps it was a matter of belief or doctrine they couldn't quite get their mind around. Perhaps it was a matter of social or economic class that put them outside of the inside circle. Perhaps it was the color of their skin, their gender, or their sexual orientation. Whatever the cause, they are bruised, wounded, and excluded.

The good news here is that many of those bruised reeds are dimly burning wicks. They are smoldering but still on fire, even if only barely. They have not given up. They are fighting for the oxygen of the Holy Spirit to ignite a smoldering ember into a new and vigorous flame. As deep and profound as their pain may be, their yearning for God, their love for Jesus, their desire to belong to a community of resurrection faith is still smoldering. In spite of their discouragement, there is just enough fire left in them to claim a morsel of hope, perhaps not hopeful, but craving it and trying to get there.

I have long believed that God has given the Episcopal Church a holy charism with respect to bruised reeds and smoldering wicks. I believe we have the gracious capacity to let those who have been burned by the church slip quietly in the back door, hide behind a column in the nave, stick their toe in the water, and be given the time and space to find their way back in. It is a frightful thing to step across the threshold of a church on a Sunday morning even under the best of circumstances. Churches that pride themselves on being warm and friendly often are not. It feels that way to the insiders and that very fact may mean it feels even more unwelcoming to a stranger. Multiply that dynamic a thousand times for someone whose heart longs to be part of the family but who has been painfully, even cruelly, rejected. Can the Episcopal Church live into the charism of making time and space for the bruised reeds and smoldering wicks?

There are those, of course, who come to our churches and need a more active, somewhat more aggressive welcome. That's fine, and that's the sort of thing one can find in a lot of churches. But if you're fighting the church's exclusion, being thrown into the deep end of the pool too quickly is not helpful. One needs a gentle entry and an unhurried journey. Healing from the pain of rejection may take months, or even years.

I once heard a bishop say that the problem with the Episcopal Church was indiscriminate inclusivity. What an incredibly stupid thing to say! Where's the welcoming, inviting, loving heart of Jesus in that? I believe we should work hard toward discriminating exclusivity! I believe that we should welcome only those for whom the Lord has died. And we should welcome them with abandon, unconditionally, and for as long as it takes for them to heal. And then, forever.

J. Neil Alexander
Dean of the School of Theology
University of the South
Sewanee, Tennessee

QUESTIONS FOR INDIVIDUALS

1. Have you ever attended a church as a guest? What was your experience? Did you feel welcomed or ignored?

2. Do you feel "seen" at your church, valued and known? If not, is there anything you can do to help facilitate connections? How can you commit to "seeing" others?

3. How often do you look around during Sunday worship or at other gatherings, intentionally seeking opportunities to talk with guests and/or newcomers?

4. What do you say when you greet a newcomer? You might consider practicing with a friend or family member so that you become more comfortable.

5. Think about your congregation and its activities. Which ones help incorporate newcomers? What role can you play in extending hospitality and welcome to new members?

QUESTIONS FOR GROUPS

1. Do your clergy, staff, and lay leaders teach, preach, and model a theology of Welcome and hospitality? In what ways? What ideas do you have for expanding this Welcome component?

2. Do the members of your congregation intentionally look for the stranger in their midst?

3. Would you say your congregation is a friendly community or is it a community of friends?

4. Who in your congregation has the gift of hospitality?

5. Does your church have an organized, comprehensive strategy and system for welcoming and following up with newcomers? If so, do the members of your vestry and leadership know the details of the system?

6. How is your welcoming system working? What needs to be added and/or changed?

RESOURCES: The appendix includes a checklist for the Welcome essential as well as some tools for implementation. For more ideas and resources, visit: www.invitewelcomeconnect. sewanee.edu

Chapter 4

CONNECT

For as in one body we have many members, and not all the members have the same function, so we, who are many, are one body in Christ, and individually we are members one of another. We have gifts that differ according to the grace given to us.

Romans 12:4-6

The ministry of lay persons is to represent Christ and his Church, to bear witness to him wherever they may be; and, according to the gifts given them, to carry on Christ's work of reconciliation in the world, and to take their place in the life, worship, and governance of the Church.

The Book of Common Prayer

When you listen generously to people they can hear the truth for themselves, often for the first time.

Rachel Naomi Remen

The Connect essential starts with offering a safe space where both newcomers and long-time members can share their stories of what brought them to your church. Then through the holy gift of listening, we help people discern their giftedness and encourage them in their journey of faith. Connect offers clear pathways to belonging where newcomers are guided in their journey of faith and into the life of the congregation, where new members are empowered and equipped to live into their baptismal covenant by offering their individual gifts and talents to God, and where we help them hear God's call in their lives. Connect gives meaning to membership, helping the newcomer answer these questions: Where do I fit in? Can I make friends in this church? Is there room for me? Does this church need me? Do I live faithfully into the gifts and talents God has given me? Can I find a place to belong and serve? Am I safe here?

Connect helps people claim their life's work as ministry, as spiritual practice, believing that their daily work can be holy sacred work. How do we as faith communities more deeply engage the people we serve? How do we help folks become more faithful stewards of the blessings of this life? How do we create safe spaces where we can truly hear each other? The Connect assessments, tools, and resources assist our congregations in answering these questions.

Connect: What Jesus Says

I did not like Mary Parmer. When we first met, if I could have engineered an escape from her, I surely would have taken it. Mary roared into my office armed with a yellow legal pad, a black felt pen, and a fierce Mississippi Baptist determination. She sat down across from me and began her inquisition. *Do Episcopalians believe we are saved by grace? Why do you baptize infants? Is Holy Communion some conjured up magic pathway to heaven? Do you people even believe in hell?* Frankly, at that moment, I really did. Growing up in the Deep South, I loathed these ecclesiastical examinations. How could I get this railing Southern Baptist out of my office?

On that day, twenty-two years ago, Mary and I were strangers, but we became friends—the very best—for we ultimately connected at a much deeper level than the entrenched certainties emanating from our separate spiritual enclaves. Our communion was forged, not so much out of agreement or compromise but rather through a gift neither Mary nor I expected. Grace ambushed us.

I do not know why we were surprised. Jesus tells his followers that friendship—real friendship—is a gift. Like our salvation and transformation in Christ, we are connected to one another through grace and not through any uber-amiability that we have construed. To that end, when Jesus announces to his disciples at the Last Supper, "No one has greater love than this, to lay down one's life for one's friends," he is not so much telling them who they are as who they will be (John

15:13). Even a cursory reading of the gospels discloses the heavy clay feet of the disciples. They demonstrate not one iota of fidelity to Jesus as he is tormented, tortured, and executed by the Roman Empire's aficionados of pain. And yet it is Christ's crucifixion and resurrection that draws the disciples into communion with God. As Paul professes a mere thirty years after the resurrection, "But now in Christ Jesus you who once were far off have been brought near by the blood of Christ" (Ephesians 2:13). The disciples don't deserve friendship with God and neither do we. As Fleming Rutledge wrote in *The Crucifixion*, the unassailable love cast from the cross has snared and drawn us into the embrace of the Trinity.

Wonderful as it is, the miracle of the cross is more expansive still. The grace that forges our friendship with God also gathers us to one another. Again, Paul, writing to Christians in a world every bit as stratified and separated as ours, declares, "There is no longer Jew or Greek, there is no longer slave or free, there is no longer male and female; for all of you are one in Christ Jesus" (Galatians 3:28). The barriers between race, gender, and class do not automatically dissipate, no matter how many cultural sensitivity and race relations seminars we take. No, the barricades that once stood so prominently between us crumble under the transformative love exhibited on the cross. Martin Luther King's "dream" was incubated in southern Sunday school rooms—both black and white. Christ causes a revolution in the hearts of those who come to know him, such that we reach across the bulwarks and become true friends.

To that end, throngs of people were drawn into the early church because of the community they experienced there. To follow the imperial cult was the safer bet and one that opened up civic and material advancement. The Stoics and Epicureans offered avenues of balance and reason. And for some, continuing in Judaism maintained family expectations and traditions. Nevertheless, only the church invited people into a living body where the radical love of the cross was an existential reality. Christ himself promised, "For where two or three are gathered in my name, I am there among them" (Matthew 18:20). Those early seekers discovered that this was not just wishful thinking but a reality into which they were immersed. No wonder the earliest church was largely a charismatic community. The Holy Spirit glued the most unlikely characters together and charged the assembly with the divine: "They devoted themselves to the apostles' teaching and fellowship, to the breaking of bread and the prayers. Awe came upon everyone, because many wonders and signs were being done by the apostles" (Acts 2:42-43).

So Mary and I were bonded together as friends, an unlikely duo if ever there was one. We were called into a terribly beleaguered parish, which Christ healed. People were drawn into that Episcopal church much like Christ drew those first seekers. Across the centuries, Christ is the one who calls us, and he is the one who connects us. People are desperately seeking real meaning and true love in their lives. Mary knows this because she, too, was bold enough to seek… even while armed with a yellow legal pad in hand. We don't need to orchestrate intricate strategies to call people into our parishes, just be faithful to intentionally invite them to be with us, lavishly welcome them into our communities when they arrive, and actually connect with them—truly get to know them and let them know us. As in all things, Christ does the heavy lifting. After all, it's his body we're talking about, and it is fueled solely by grace.

Patrick Gahan
Rector, Christ Episcopal Church
San Antonio, Texas

The essential of Connect can be described in a variety of ways: Giving meaning to membership; Empowering laity for ministry; Closing the back door; Belonging. But the essence of this essential is love — love for one another is the thread that runs through this ministry. The Rev. Gay Clark Jennings, now president of the House of Deputies of the Episcopal Church, told me about a sermon she wrote in 1991 entitled "Invite Welcome Love." At the end of her handwritten sermon were these words: "Our church is certainly messy with its richness of people, its variety of nationalities and races, its theological understandings, its interpretations of scripture and tradition. In the midst of the mess, we are called to invite, welcome, and love. We are called to know that Jesus is with us, a calm presence in the midst of the storm, guiding and directing us, and telling us not to be afraid."

> We are called to know that Jesus is with us, a calm presence in the midst of the storm, guiding and directing us, and telling us not to be afraid.
>
> - Gay Clark Jennings

Long before the Invite Welcome Connect ministry took shape, Gay Clark Jennings articulated the key principle: love. The Connect essential is all about love and relationship. God created us in love, and we exist in the image of a relational God. Our spiritual and human connections give our lives meaning. Neuroscience research confirms that humans are hardwired for connection. In an interview, Dr. Amy Banks, director of Advanced Training at the Jean Baker Miller Training Institute at the Wellesley Centers for Women and an instructor of psychiatry at Harvard Medical School, says:

> *Neuroscience is confirming that our nervous systems want us to connect with other human beings. A good example of this is mirror neurons, which are located*

throughout the brain and help us read other people's feelings and actions. They may be the neurological underpinnings of empathy — when two people are in conversation they are stimulating each other's mirror neuron system. Not only will this lead to movement in similar muscles of the face (so the expressions are similar) but it also allows each to feel what the other is feeling. This is an automatic, moment-to-moment resonance that connects us. There have been studies that look at emotions in human beings such as disgust, shame, happiness, where the exact same areas of the brain light up in the listener who is reading the feelings of the person talking. We are, literally, hardwired to connect.

We are, literally, hardwired to connect

- Amy Banks

Given this scientific evidence, we should pay close attention to helping newcomers connect with God and others. And we shouldn't be surprised that if people do not find connections and relationships, they go out the back door in search of this deep longing!

I have come to believe that the Connect essential in Invite Welcome Connect may be the most important element of this entire ministry: Members will not invite others to a church or community that they do not feel excited about or invested in. Perhaps the Connect essential needs to be practiced first within a congregation so that people have something to invite and welcome people to with joy and excitement.

When I came to my current parish, it had declined in numbers and had lost a sense of growing in discipleship. Before we could look beyond our doors to bring people in, we needed to create an environment that gave them deeply spiritual reasons to stay. We turned to Invite Welcome Connect to give us a solid foundation for a deliberate and strategic plan for evangelism and hospitality efforts, but we also focused internally on the important Connect piece to make sure Christ was central in our journey.

We established a team of people who walked with newcomers for their first year in the congregation—inviting them to events, suggesting ministries that they might be perfect for, and remembering them in their prayers. We also took the important step of connecting with people who had been there for years but had not yet joined a ministry or discipleship effort. We developed programs and offerings that helped to build a life centered on Christ—efforts like Bible studies, Lenten programs, community yoga classes, and Christian formation opportunities for all ages.

The real beauty of the Connect essential is helping members realize that the more they connect with their church, the more they grow with Christ. And the more they grow with Christ, the more excited they become to welcome people in. Thanks to the Holy Spirit, transformation is happening because people are more connected with their church than ever before and are bursting with joy to share this with others.

Hillary D. Raining
Rector
St. Christopher's Episcopal Church
Gladwyne, Pennsylvania

The deep truth of Connect is the sacred act of listening. When we relate to those around us by hearing their stories and then connecting them with others, we build the loving communities of faith God intends for us to live fully into. Before clergy and lay leaders tell newcomers what the church can offer and do for them, they must first listen to the newcomers' stories, finding out what brought them to visit the church in the first place. This suggestion extends to long-time members of our congregations as well, especially those members who have never been involved in ministry. Perhaps the reason for this is that we have not taken the time to intentionally listen to their stories, helping them discern their giftedness and find their place of ministry. Dietrich Bonhoeffer in *Life Together* speaks directly to this subject, "The first service that one owes to others in the fellowship consists of listening to them. Just as love of God begins with listening to his word, so the beginning of love for our brothers and sisters is learning to listen to them." Lynne Baab's *The Power of Listening* and Keith Anderson's *A Spirituality of Listening* are excellent resources and provide reflective exercises and tools for learning listening skills for individuals and congregations.

> Just as love of God begins with listening to his word, so the beginning of love for our brothers and sisters is learning to listen to them.
>
> - Dietrich Bonhoeffer

Essential to connection is true belonging. Historically, the Episcopal Church has waited for newcomers to make some sort of commitment to membership before reaching out to include them in activities of the church. At St. Mary's Episcopal Church in Cypress, Texas, we reversed that process. We believe people don't join churches without experiencing meaningful connection first and that must be done with joy, respect, and intention.

Cypress is a suburb of Houston, and many people commute hours every day to and from work. Offering a "newcomer class" seemed like another burden on already busy lives. Pushing people toward service was premature. After a period of discernment, the Seekers Forum was born. The Forum is a small group with one clergy, two lay members, and about eight newcomers who may or may not have decided to join the church. Designed as a hybrid of in-person gatherings and online discussion, the Forum is an exploration in relationship. There is no Sunday morning requirement, and it works for people on the go. The goal of the Forum is to create a safe place for sharing, believing that sharing our stories is a critical path to belonging.

The Forum's in-person activities occur in locations other than a classroom setting to cultivate an environment of openness and vulnerability. Kicking off the group on a Saturday afternoon in a current member's home, members of the Forum share a bit of their faith journey by discussing how they first came to church and specifically to St. Mary's. The afternoon continues with participants drawing questions out of a bag; the questions are designed to spark conversation and create connections. They include topics such as: "What was your best vacation?" or "What is the biggest change in your life this year?" Clergy and members gain valuable insight when newcomers share their experiences of St. Mary's, and often this gathering plants the seeds for meaningful relationships. Stories are honored by listening respectfully and maintaining confidentiality. Tears are not uncommon.

After these initial meet and greets, the Forum small groups ponder topics in a private Facebook group for four weeks. We answer questions like "What's on your bucket list?" and discuss deeper topics such as answers to prayer and life lessons. Another bonus: newcomers get to know priests as people and not only as worship leaders.

After the Facebook sharing period, a Celebration Dinner is held in a home on a Saturday evening. Spouses and children are invited to attend with the participants. The evening includes playing an interactive game as well as gathering feedback about the experience. Newcomers often say they have never had such a profound encounter with a church community. For introverts, the Seekers Forum is a safe way to get to know others; for extroverts, it's another opportunity to build relationships.

St. Mary's has held seven Seekers Forums so far, and the feedback has been overwhelmingly positive. Participants build relationships quickly and become engaged in parish life on their terms. When you find yourself asking the same old question, "How can we get our newcomers to attend this class?" I encourage you to stop and reframe the question, instead asking, "How can we meet our newcomers' need for belonging?" This is the birthplace of innovation. Jesus was a change agent. While he did not abandon tradition, many of his actions were new and unorthodox. The Holy Spirit gives us inspiration to create, experiment, and evolve. And the fruits are truly life-changing.

Molly Wills Carnes
Lay Leader
St. Mary's Episcopal Church
Cypress, Texas

Empowering the laity for ministry is a crucial aspect of the Connect essential, and I've found I must unpack this principle quite often. Empowering laity for ministry is not about clergy giving away their power; rather, it is about clergy (and others) helping people discover the power God has given them to do the ministry they have been called to as laity. A few years ago at a clergy conference, I posed this question to two young clergy: "Do you have a problem with the word 'empowering' as in 'empowering laity for ministry'? If so, please say more!" One of the priests explained, "Empowering can be liberating or paternalistic based on who is using it and how it is being used. It needs to be clearly defined before you use it." As we discussed this phrase, the three of us decided on this working description for empowering laity for ministry: "Recognizing the real presence of God's Holy Spirit in the other, equipping them to claim their own power."

One Sunday morning in the fall of 2002, Jack Aulbaugh, a new member at St. Stephen's Beaumont, came up to me during coffee hour with an idea for a ministry initiative. He suggested that we invite other churches in the area to cook our favorite foods and sell tickets like the restaurant association had done for many years. After some discussion, we decided to check with Some Other Place, a local ecumenical organization that provided a soup kitchen, clothing, and essentials to the indigent population, to see if they would be interested in this concept as a fundraiser.

In August 2017, Some Other Place held their 15th Annual "Tasting for Some Other Place" at the Beaumont Civic Center. The event has become one of the biggest public parties Beaumont has ever seen, with more than 50 food vendors. The fundraising goal in 2017 was $100,000—covering a month's worth of the organization's budget to provide needed resources of food, clothing, and emergency services. Empowering the laity for ministry is the vital lesson of this story. What if we had said to Jack: "This would be such a big undertaking. I don't think we should attempt it…blah, blah, blah…" Any response other than "Let's give it a try" might have sent the idea to the trash bin.

Church of the Nativity, Scottsdale, was growing beyond the point where we could keep track of all the people simply by intuition. As we grew, we discovered that we needed to create intentional systems to help people connect to each other and the parish.

That's where the shepherd program came in. We trained a group of people with special gifts of hospitality and pastoral care as shepherds. Each shepherd had twelve to twenty families in his or her flock. The shepherds' duties began with welcoming and getting to know their assigned newcomers through phone calls, coffee or lunch dates, etc. This gave an extra level of welcome beyond the regular pastoral and newcomer ministry contacts.

Then, as the shepherds got to know their newcomers, the shepherd could help them get connected with ministries that suited their interests. The shepherd also introduced them to others with similar interests, especially since we tried to assign shepherd groups by common interests. The shepherds periodically gathered their groups together for social time to help people make friends.

The third major area of responsibility for shepherds was to keep an eye out for lost sheep. If someone didn't show up to church for three weeks in a row, the shepherd gave the missing folks a call. Sometimes this call was simply a welcome reminder to busy folks that they were missed. Sometimes such calls would discover pastoral issues that the shepherds relayed to the clergy for follow-up. The shepherd program helped people get connected and helped close the back door that can widen as a church grows.

Susan Brown Snook
Canon to the Ordinary
Diocese of Oklahoma

Another significant element of the Connect essential is the importance of helping newcomers and long-time members alike understand how God has shaped them for ministry, thus helping them connect with the ministries that match their spiritual gifts, strengths, and talents. My particular journey into the Episcopal Church involved an epiphany of sorts around this subject. I entered the Episcopal Church in 1996 and shortly thereafter took a spiritual gifts inventory in a Community of Hope class. My primary gift is exhortation, defined as the ability to encourage others to grow emotionally and spiritually. My epiphany came as I recalled that an inventory fifteen years prior had resulted in the same primary gift, but instead of capitalizing on that gift, I had been asked to teach ninth-grade girls. After a few months I felt like a total failure, and I managed to get out of teaching the class as quickly as possible, moving on to other ministries that fully utilized my gifts, strengths, and talents.

We are called to live into the gospel of Jesus Christ with the unique giftedness given to each one of us. Richard Rohr writes

> All we can give back and all God wants from any of us is to humbly and proudly return the product that we have been given—which is ourselves!
>
> - Richard Rohr

in his book *Falling Upward*, "All we can give back and all God wants from any of us is to humbly and proudly return the product that we have been given—which is ourselves!" Discovering my spiritual giftedness became a pivotal moment in my faith journey. It was the beginning of God calling me to be the authentic woman God created me to be, rather than conforming to someone else's image of me.

I can't stress this enough: It is critical for us to understand how God has gifted and shaped each one of us, then for us to discern and understand how we might put our individual giftedness to best use. You have been given gifts and talents that are needed by the world around you, and my encouragement to you is to pray for God's guidance in discernment of your gifts and calling. People burn out fairly quickly if they are attempting to do ministry that does not match their individual spiritual giftedness, and it is our job as a church to help people discern this important part of their spiritual lives and journey of faith.

I remember my first Connect committee meeting at St. John's Episcopal Church in Tallahassee, Florida. I was one of two people on the committee who had recently joined the church. We were asked to tell the committee about our experience. I went first and told the group about my unbelievable first day at St. John's. I told the group about the parishioner who greeted me on the sidewalk outside of the church. This parishioner had attended an earlier service and was on the way home. Upon discovering I was a visitor, the person stopped, welcomed me, and escorted me to the church. I spoke about being invited to see the historic bell tower and about being invited to have coffee by another parishioner and a clergy member after the service. In the months following that first day, I received an invitation to become an usher and was invited to brunch, dinner, and a variety of other church functions. The other relatively new member spoke next, and I was surprised to hear that her experience was totally different from mine.

We asked ourselves the question: Why were the two experiences so different? We joined the same church around the same time. We listened to the same sermons, listened to the same amazing choir, and attended some of the same church functions. In the end, the answer was simple and became the framework of our Connect ministry. The personal interactions between me and other parishioners established a connection that made me feel like there was a place for me at St. John's. I felt I had found not just a place to worship but a church family.

Our committee identified early on that for this ministry to be successful, it would require getting the entire parish involved. To start, we held a forum and we shared the two different new member experiences. We wanted to show the impact that making a personal connection can have on someone who is walking through the church doors for the first time. We encouraged members to start offering this type of hospitality. We also established a series of events that provided a way to bring newcomers together in a comfortable setting for discussions with members of the clergy and other parishioners.

Today, these events include clergy-led new member classes, newcomer luncheons, and newcomer receptions. The newcomer events provide opportunities for newcomers to ask questions about the Christian faith, hear St. John's story, and learn about our many church ministries, as well as meet other parishioners and newcomers. The Connect committee members each make personal invitations to newcomers for these events and further participate by attending, listening, and talking to the newcomers in an effort to discover their interests so that they can help them get connected at St. John's.

The results of these efforts have been amazing, and it is truly rewarding to hear people say that they are joining the church because of the efforts of this ministry. A year and a half after starting this ministry, ninety-nine people have gone through the new members class and decided to join St. John's. The Connect ministry at St. John's is truly making an impact on the church and the people who walk through our doors every day.

Brooks Butler
Invite Welcome Connect Chair
Lay Leader, St. John's Episcopal Church
Tallahassee, Florida

As the Body of Christ, we must become seriously intentional and systematic about living out the vital essential of Connect. Critical to this ministry is the development and implementation of an intentional system for connecting newcomers, modeling deep and holy listening in our conversations, and building clear pathways to belonging. Empowering laity for ministry by assisting in discernment of gifts, strengths, and vocations can be a game changer in our communities of faith. Recognition, affirmation, and celebration of lay ministries validate the critical ministry of the laity, and clergy will not regret making this a priority. The Connect essential helps close the back doors of our churches — so that people stop leaving as fast as they enter. When we practice the essential of Connect, we will experience transformation and our communities of faith will live into God's dream for us all.

PRAYER

Gracious Lord, thank you for the gifts and talents you have bestowed upon each of us. We invite you to stir up these God-given gifts. Give us grace to bear witness to them. Help us claim our life's work as ministry, as holy sacred work. *Amen.*

QUESTIONS FOR INDIVIDUALS

1. What brought you to your current church? If possible, think about your first few visits. What (and who) helped you connect with the congregation?

2. How often do you invite others to share with you their stories of faith? How can you practice the sacred act of listening?

3. Do you feel empowered to exercise your ministry? If not, what is holding you back?

4. What are your spiritual gifts? Consider taking a spiritual gifts inventory (there are several options online) and reflect upon your gifts and how they might best be used in your current circumstance.

QUESTIONS FOR GROUPS

1. Do your clergy, staff, and lay leaders teach, preach, and model Connect, helping people discern their giftedness (vocation), and then empower, equip, entrust, and affirm them for ministry?

2. Do you have an intentional system of tracking and following up with every single newcomer? What is your process for connecting newcomers into ministry at your church?

3. Given that the deep truth of Connect is the sacred act of listening, does your congregation offer any resources/

classes for listening skills? What creative ways can you offer to deeply listen to people's stories?

4. Can you identify the members of your congregation who are "connectors"—people who naturally have a gift for connecting others?

5. Given that newcomer ministry needs to be a team effort, how do clergy and/or lay volunteers interact with newcomers?

6. What are your congregation's pathways to belonging? Does your church offer a clear membership pathway, teaching the importance of Episcopal rites of initiation, e.g., baptism, confirmation, and reception?

7. What process is in place for empowering laity for ministry? Does your church have a variety of resources/methods/classes to assist people in discerning their God-given giftedness for ministry? Does your church have written descriptions of all lay ministries in your church?

8. In what ways do you communicate ongoing up-to-date information about lay ministries to your newcomers and congregation?

9. Does your congregation have exit conversations with people who leave your church?

RESOURCES: The appendix includes a checklist for the Connect essential as well as some tools for implementation. For more ideas and resources, visit: www.invitewelcomeconnect.sewanee.edu

Chapter 5

CREATIVITY

*May you experience each day as a sacred gift woven around
the heart of wonder.*
John O'Donohue
Irish poet and priest

*If I were to wish for anything, I should not wish for wealth and
power, but for the passionate sense of what can be, for the
eye which, ever young and ardent, sees the possible. Pleasure
disappoints, possibility never. And what wine is so sparkling,
what so fragrant, what so intoxicating as possibility!*
Søren Kierkegaard
Danish philosopher and theologian

Everyone is born with imagination, and small children are
especially experts. As a middle child growing up in Natchez,
Mississippi, I spent most of my days playing alone—my two
older brothers were playmates and my younger identical twin
sisters had each other. Besides playing jacks and reading,

one of my favorite pastimes was creating little towns around mud puddles and in the midst of the roots of the old oak trees surrounding our house. My world was full of wonder in those days, a place of endless possibilities, and the power of my imagination served me well. Imagination in a child is one thing, but imagination is not always highly valued in adults. We are much too practical to imagine villages around mud puddles. Yet I am convinced that we are being called to remember and cultivate the power of our imagination and creativity as we build God's church.

Just as Jesus models seeing the other and holy hospitality for us, he also models creativity. His parables and actions are chock-full of creative wonder, whimsy, wit, and wisdom, all rolled into stories that touch our souls and cause us to ponder the creative possibilities a life of faith can offer. Consider the wonder of the mustard seed, the smallest of seeds, growing into a tree filled with bird nests, or ponder the whimsical nature of Jesus' insistence that the children be allowed to come unto him. Think about the wit of Jesus as he tells Zacchaeus to come down from the tree so that he can invite himself to his house. And who can argue with the deep wisdom in the creative parable of the prodigal son?

God is the giver of all things, and the Holy Spirit instills the gift of deep wells of creativity within each of us, but we must open ourselves up to this potential for our lives. Invite Welcome Connect invites us to be co-creators with God as we imagine with wonder, whimsy, wit, and wisdom the possibilities for ourselves and for our congregations.

In 2012, Holy Comforter was a struggling pastoral-size congregation in the northern suburbs of Houston. Since then, Holy Comforter has doubled in size. With such a steady influx of visitors, we realized that we needed to implement a more structured process of welcome for our newcomers. We began with a creative solution: Newcomer Cafe. On regularly scheduled Sunday mornings, our newcomer minister and I sit down with everybody who has started coming to Holy Comforter in the previous six weeks. We use this opportunity to share with newcomers the core values, mission, and vision of our church. But more importantly, Newcomer Cafe is a set-aside time for us to hear from newcomers.

Sometimes when we try to welcome newcomers into our congregations, we simply talk too much. Part of what we do at Newcomer Cafe is intentionally listen to our newcomers. What are they looking for? How did they find Holy Comforter? How do they hope to grow closer to Jesus by participating in the life of our church?

Importantly, Newcomer Cafe takes place at church on Sunday mornings rather than in a home during the evening. For many of our visitors, it took a lot of courage just to come to church on a Sunday morning. Inviting them into the home of a vestry person or staff member would be far too intimidating. Second, those newcomers with young children can use our nursery without having to schedule babysitters.

The real key to Newcomer Cafe, however, is that visitors to Holy Comforter get to see that they are not alone. If you are visiting a church, it can seem that you are the only one who is new. By gathering all the newcomers together at once, it is obvious they are not alone, and it provides an opportunity for immediate connection with others.

Jimmy Abbott
Rector, Holy Comforter Episcopal Church
Spring, Texas

As I shared earlier, I grew up Southern Baptist in Mississippi and following a divorce, I opened a business. My story during that time, though, is one of an imagined life. Someone encouraged me to read *The Artist's Way* by Julia Cameron, and this book was pivotal in my faith journey. It helped me envision a new reality for myself and to dream forward what my life could be, post-divorce.

I knew deep down that my soul was in dire need of healing, so I spent a good deal of time imagining a life of reconciliation and wholeness, family and friends, and a meaningful, life-giving vocation, even though I was, at the time, a divorced Southern Baptist woman, wounded and full of self-doubt, who had not finished her college education. Did I worry during this troubling time in my life? Of course. Did I have faith God would bring healing to my soul? I didn't know for sure. Did I believe God would somehow bring me through these challenges to the other side? Yes. But I had no idea what that future would hold. As the English poet John Keats wrote, "I am certain of

I am certain of nothing but the holiness of the heart's affections and the truth of the imagination.

- John Keats

nothing but the holiness of the heart's affections and the truth of the imagination."

Of course, God works in wonderous ways, beyond our imagining, and now I am helping others in this ministry of invitation, welcome, and connection. One thing I know for sure from this journey: Imagination does more than affect us. It effects change in our lives. Well-known Episcopal priest and author Barbara Brown Taylor suggests in her book, *The Preaching Life*, that the church's central task is an imaginative one. "Holy imagination is a way of seeing—a way of living—that requires a certain loosening of the grip, a willingness to be surprised, confused, amazed by the undreamt-of ways that God chooses to be revealed to us. To find the extraordinary hidden in the ordinary, we are called to participate in God's own imagination—to see ourselves, our neighbors, and our world through God's eyes, full of possibility, full of promise, ready to be transformed...because God is not through with us yet."

I had only recently read the creative book on visual literacy, *The Doodle Revolution*, when I had the pleasure of keynoting the Episcopal Church in Europe's annual parish leadership event. The gift of creativity is expressed in numerous ways, and doodling is something I observe at almost every Invite Welcome Connect workshop I lead, including this one in Munich, Germany, where several women doodled throughout the day. A few short weeks after returning from Europe, I received a kind note from Alison Wale, from Saint Just-en-Chevalet, France, with a zentangle Celtic design she had created especially for this ministry. What a gift!

Christian apologist and author C. S. Lewis provides wonderful examples of using imagination as a tool for strengthening and deepening faith. His conversion to Christianity was prompted by what he called the baptism of his imagination through reading George MacDonald's *Phantastes*. In *The Screwtape Letters*, Lewis describes the human soul as a series of three concentric circles: the outermost as imagination, the middle as intellect, and the innermost as will. Paul F. Ford writes in his *Companion to Narnia* that Lewis felt strongly that children's imaginations should be encouraged and nourished. For Lewis, the purpose of a story is to set "before our imagination something that has always baffled the intellect." The fantastic world of Narnia leads us on a journey of faith by opening a sacred door of imagination. God knows what can happen when we open those sacred doors in our lives and in our congregations.

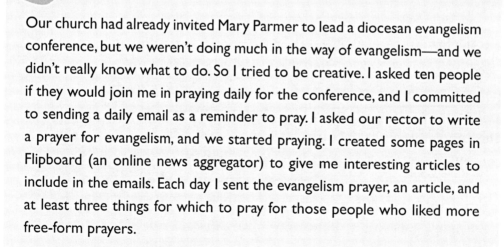

Our church had already invited Mary Parmer to lead a diocesan evangelism conference, but we weren't doing much in the way of evangelism—and we didn't really know what to do. So I tried to be creative. I asked ten people if they would join me in praying daily for the conference, and I committed to sending a daily email as a reminder to pray. I asked our rector to write a prayer for evangelism, and we started praying. I created some pages in Flipboard (an online news aggregator) to give me interesting articles to include in the emails. Each day I sent the evangelism prayer, an article, and at least three things for which to pray for those people who liked more free-form prayers.

Somebody in your church can do this. I know, because I was that somebody in mine. The hardest part was working up the courage to ask ten people to agree to pray every day. We didn't stop when the conference arrived, and I've continued the daily emails in the months since the conference in April 2017. Our email list has grown to thirty people. Guess what happens when nearly half of your congregation is thinking about evangelism every day? We built a new Welcome Center and added a dozen new members in the first year.

I use all kinds of resources, from C.S. Lewis to the Baptist tradition (they are a wellspring of information on evangelism because they are intentional about it!). Around the holidays, I use YouTube videos of music and pageantry, and from time to time, I include cartoons. Once in a while I share an experience of my own, but I think if these emails get preachy, they will go unread.

If I miss a day, I miss a day, but I put out about 320-340 emails a year. I have several readers who go to work early but like to read the emails before work. I try to (and usually, but not always) get the emails out by 7 a.m.

Hal Foss
Lay Leader
Memorial Church of the Good Shepherd
Parkersburg, West Virginia

WISDOM BEGINS IN WONDER

In the early years of developing Invite Welcome Connect, I read two critical books that helped shape my ministry: Thomas Edward Frank's *The Soul of the Congregation: An Invitation to Congregational Reflection* and Diana Butler Bass's *Christianity for the Rest of Us: How the Neighborhood Church Is Transforming the Faith.* Both stress the value of appreciating every congregation's unique culture and their embodiment of courage, creativity, imagination, and risk—and recognizing possibilities for ministry derived from these values and strengths.

As I began sharing this ministry of Invite Welcome Connect with congregations in the Diocese of Texas, I particularly enjoyed working with the smaller churches, helping them articulate their uniqueness and opening them up to creative possibilities for ministry. Bass writes that "lively faith is not located in buildings, programs, organizations, and structures… rather, spiritual vitality lives in human beings: It is located in the heart of God's people and the communities they form."

I am immensely grateful for the opportunity to have been in relationship with many soulful, vital communities of faith while developing Invite Welcome Connect. What a joy it is to discover hidden gems of delight, creativity, and play, including:

- A church chicken named Sister Paulina (St. Paul's, Houston), which kept pecking on the parish hall door windows throughout the entire workshop!

- Creative, spontaneous fundraising and community involvement ideas at a *dominis ecclesia* (house church) filled with treasures from all over the world, including the original pews from an old 1866 nave (St. Joseph's, Salado)

- A glowing, excited newcomer who shared her story of being welcomed at her first Episcopal worship service: "It's as if the Holy Spirit was hanging from the ceiling, you know, like George Clooney or Batman, hovering over the nave, welcoming us all to church!" (St. James, LaGrange)

As I began taking Invite Welcome Connect to congregations around the country, I realized I needed a concrete way to engage folks in imaginative, creative work, a playful place where they could let their imagination fly. I began following each short teaching on Invite Welcome Connect with small group work. In these idea-generating groups (baby think tanks) my instructions are to use the Invite Welcome Connect resources as prompts for creative experiments—and to put aside any conversation about how much it might cost, how much time it would take, etc. Each small group is given a set of multicolored Post-it notes and multicolored markers, with instructions to write down each idea on a separate Post-it note. After about thirty minutes, one person from each group reports the ideas, and we post them on nearby walls or windows, creating a mosaic of creative and imaginative ideas. I've discovered that this exercise is generative, freeing people to use their imaginations and creativity in a way they've rarely done in the context of the church. At the end of the day's workshop, I suggest that folks ponder and pray about which of the three essentials— Invite Welcome Connect—makes their hearts sing, and then I recommend that they create teams in their congregation to begin putting legs under the ideas generated.

In her book *Holy Curiosity*, psychology professor Amy Hollingsworth addresses creativity, writing that creativity isn't possible without holy curiosity about our own lives and the possibilities and patterns that reside there. We ask ourselves,

"What is my passion? What makes my heart sing? What burns on my heart?" Reflecting on these questions quite often energizes us and helps us live incarnational lives.

I believe with my whole heart that the reason this work has been transformational across the different cultures/contexts of parishes in rural and city settings is due to our reliance on the Spirit's guiding as we engage folks in the small group work. Trusting the Holy Spirit enables creativity. And giving people a chance to use their God-given gifts and holy imaginations in arriving at simple ideas and solutions is powerful. We give these small groups a creative place where their imagination can fly, and a buy-in takes place that would not happen without their creative individual and collective input. Not only do folks leave the Invite Welcome Connect workshops with their heads bursting with ideas, but they also leave energized and excited about the possibilities to come!

Engaging in the Invite Welcome Connect ministry opens people up to possibility and playful creativity, to the idea that an important part of our vocation as humans is not only to use the gifts God gives each one of us but also to tap into the amazing energy of the imaginative, creative mind God gives us. Saying yes to God's gift of creativity is our gift back to God!

St. Stephen's Episcopal Church is an affluent rural parish located in the historic district of Oxford, North Carolina, just north of Raleigh/Durham. Established in 1823, St. Stephen's has served an important role in Oxford for nearly two hundred years. Most notably today, the church is known for its local outreach and mission efforts.

With a town population of about 11,000, it would be easy to assume that attracting new members to the church is slow and difficult. However, Oxford tends to draw new folks every month or two from the Northeast who know something about our church tradition — people who want to live near the big cities but love the idealistic comfort of small-town living. Many of the visitors are church-shopping, and they report St. Stephen's parishioners to be friendly and welcoming.

As a pastoral-size congregation, we do not have the resources of the larger churches, but there are creative ways to accomplish our goals and mission. After hearing Mary Parmer speak at the 2015 convention for the Diocese of North Carolina, my senior warden and I both knew our parishioners needed to hear her enthusiastic message. However, we knew Mary was in high demand and the chances of scheduling her for a visit to our parish were slim. So we creatively organized a Sunday morning presentation via the Invite Welcome Connect website. We presented segments of a video presentation she made in another diocese and then had our own discussion and examination over the course of five Sundays. The presentations were intergenerational and provided an opportunity for us to closely examine who we were, what was working, and where we could make some changes.

During the course of the Sunday mornings, we were all moved by the testimony of a new member of the parish, Jerry. He stood up and shared what had made him feel invited, welcomed, and connected. Jerry shared the experience of pulling up to the church one Sunday morning for the 8 a.m. service and the struggle he felt within himself to step out of the car and walk to the entrance.

Once he stepped out of the car and made his way to the front steps, an older couple crossed his path. Jerry said, "If it had not been for this couple and what they did, I am not sure I would have proceeded through the doors." The couple welcomed him to St. Stephen's, introduced themselves, and invited him to sit with them during the service. In addition, they offered some guidance on the nature of the service. This calmed his fears. As Jerry said, "The key for me in the first visit was that I did not feel smothered or pressured…just invited and welcomed." Jerry soon connected with our Church Life ministry and now serves in areas that speak to his interests. He found a home at St. Stephen's Church because of one couple's open spirit of hospitality.

Out of this self-examining work, we created a two-person team from the vestry whose job was to focus on Invite and Welcome. We created a friendlier welcome card for the pews and a welcome package that included a coffee cup, information on our parish, and a few extra treats.

I agree with Mary: Invite Welcome Connect is not a program. It is a series of organized resources that, when authentically engaged, offer a church and its people an opportunity to examine themselves and find a better way to live into the questions we are always asking at St. Stephen's: "Who is our neighbor? And how can we better invite and welcome them home?" I believe we continue to make progress in the areas of invite, welcome, and connect because we have taken these resources and customized them to our current context and setting.

James L. Pahl Jr.
Rector, St. Stephen's Episcopal Church
Oxford, North Carolina

> *The imagination is like a lantern. It illuminates the inner landscapes of our life and helps us discover their secret archaeologies. When our eyes are graced with wonder, the world reveals its wonders to us.*
>
> *- John O'Donohue*

Imagination is the great friend of possibility, writes John O'Donohue in *Beauty: The Invisible Embrace.* And nothing opens the mind like the glimpse of a new possibility. Through imagination, we begin to discover a whole new sense of God, O'Donohue writes. "The imagination is like a lantern. It illuminates the inner landscapes of our life and helps us discover their secret archaeologies. When our eyes are graced with wonder, the world reveals its wonders to us."

Wonder. Play. Imagination. Possibility. Creativity. These are all gifts from God and need to be honored and utilized as we implement the ministry of Invite Welcome Connect. Every congregation in the Episcopal Church has a unique culture, and our task as clergy and lay leaders is to help unearth the gifts of people in our congregations and empower them for mission, ministry, and creative possibilities. My passion is to help each congregation articulate its uniqueness, recalling an old Alban Institute booklet's reminder that our job is to help folks "spell Episcopal with the alphabet of their own soul." Every single Episcopal congregation, no matter the size, has within it immense resources for imagination and creativity. We simply need to create an environment in our congregations where creativity is honored, and we need clergy and lay leaders who take the challenge of creativity seriously.

Clergy and lay leaders who are open to the creative processes of Invite Welcome Connect have seen the most success with this work. Brené Brown writes in her book *Daring Greatly,* "Vulnerability is the birthplace of innovation, creativity, and change." This ministry requires clergy and lay leaders willing to be vulnerable—inspired risk-takers with the moral courage to risk failure for the sake of the gospel and who will put aside a philosophy of no. We need to ask God for courage, for the heart to think outside the box, and the desire to recreate, reenvision, and reimagine our ministries. Then, and only then, can we be real change agents for the glory of God.

Vulnerability is the birthplace of innovation, creativity, and change.

- Brené Brown

PRAYER

Dear Lord, grant us courage and imagination this day. Open our hearts to creativity and possibility. Fill our souls with your unfailing grace. Help us live into our calling to be faithful communities of love and relationship, to be living monuments of God's strength and grace. *Amen.*

QUESTIONS FOR INDIVIDUALS

1. Do you stifle imagination and originality in yourself? In others?

2. We all have creativity and imagination within us, even if we don't think of ourselves as creative or imaginative. How might you access the rich well of imagination within you?

3. Do you have the courage to step outside your comfort zone and confront any fears you might have around creativity?

QUESTIONS FOR GROUPS

1. What are the creative ways you are engaging newcomers and long-time members to find their place of ministry in your community of faith?

2. How do you deeply and creatively engage the people you serve in ministry?

3. Putting aside limitations of time and money, imagine what you hope your church and community will look and act like in a year, in five years, in twenty years. What creative actions can you take to move toward those dreams?

Chapter 6

OBSTACLES & OPPORTUNITIES

Now to him who by the power at work within us is able to accomplish abundantly far more than all we can ask or imagine.

Ephesians 3:20

Embracing and implementing the ministry of Invite Welcome Connect will have its challenges. Change always does. The obstacles will vary according to location, context, culture, and personality. While it is important to know that there will be road bumps, you're not alone in these challenges, and often, the obstacle raises the curtain to reveal an opportunity.

Complacency is a great challenge for Episcopal congregations today, and it might be our prevailing sin. This complacency is particularly challenging in the context of newcomer ministry.

We often think of ourselves as a friendly community when in reality we are a community of friends. Observe, if you will, any average Sunday morning coffee hour and you will see people visiting primarily with friends, not the stranger in the room.

Complacency is defined as "a feeling of smug satisfaction with your own abilities or situation that prevents you from trying harder," and scripture is filled with warnings against it. In the Gospel of Matthew, Jesus cautions, "And everyone who hears these words of mine and does not act on them will be like a foolish man who built his house on sand." Or consider Revelation 3:16, which says, "So, because you are lukewarm, and neither cold nor hot, I am about to spit you out of my mouth."

> So, because you are lukewarm, and neither cold nor hot, I am about to spit you out of my mouth.
>
> - Revelation 3:16

C. S. Lewis explores the sin of complacency in his satirical masterpiece, *The Screwtape Letters*. Screwtape, assistant to "Our Father Below," pens these words to his nephew, Wormwood:

> *Some ages are lukewarm and complacent, and then it is our business to soothe them yet faster asleep…We want the Church to be small not only that fewer men may know the Enemy but also that those who do may acquire the uneasy intensity and the defensive self-righteousness of a secret society or clique…The road to Hell is the gradual one – the gentle slope, soft underfoot, without sudden turnings, without milestones, without signposts.*

Clearly the evil one prefers that Christians remain apathetic and lackadaisical about their faith, fearful and hopeless. Confronting complacency in the context of newcomer ministry begins with awareness; the next step is to prayerfully, intentionally examine the essentials of Invite Welcome Connect. With a focus on evangelism, hospitality, and empowering laity for ministry, we challenge the sin of complacency and open our communities of faith to vast opportunities for ministry.

The challenges to implementing many of the changes that result from engaging in Invite Welcome Connect are both institutional and human. Having spent time considering the ways we could be more welcoming and inclusive as a congregation, we began the more challenging work of implementation. Mary Parmer had reminded us of the call to be a community of invitation and inclusion, but we also had to face our own roadblocks to that calling.

The conversation around welcoming young families with children is a good example of this type of obstacle. No one expressed any objection or concern about having more children at our services; in fact, the congregation has a thriving church school. The truth that we needed to attract a younger generation who would love the church as we did was not lost on anyone. However, once we began to be more intentional about welcoming young families, we ran into our own roadblocks.

Perhaps some people imagined that the young children would be so awestruck by the beauty of our church building, the magnificence of our liturgy, and the eloquence of the sermon, that they would be struck mute. But of course, when young families started coming, they brought normal, noisy children as well.

It got to a point where the vestry considered putting an additional pledge card in our stewardship materials, asking members to pledge that they would not turn around in church and glare at anyone under 18 who was making noise. We didn't actually do this; having the conversation was as important for moving forward as any action we could take.

The challenges of change will always be rooted in the reality of experience and our hopes and dreams. It may be that we do not pursue every suggestion for change or that we are willing to live with our current circumstance once change begins. We also might become willing to stretch beyond our comfort levels, to imagine and practice a new way of being church. The Invite Welcome Connect discernment process has enough structure to identify common goals, establish a process for change, and then implement those new practices. The process of inclusion is at the heart of this ministry, and we are called to live changed and changing lives as the people of God.

Richard McKeon
Rector, Episcopal Church of the Messiah
Rhinebeck, New York

Many congregations face serious challenges of inaction and inertia. We might talk (a lot) about the importance of invitation and hospitality but at the end of the day, our actions speak louder than our words. It is not what we say, teach or preach — it is what we do that speaks loudest! Do we see Christ in the newcomers who walk in our doors? And more importantly, do they see Christ in us?

In many ways, inaction goes hand-in-hand with complacency, but the inaction I'm identifying here is a refusal to follow through. As lay and clergy leaders, are we modeling what we say, preach, or teach? How many times have we personally invited someone to church? How often have we entered a room of people in our congregation and spent time visiting with friends and acquaintances rather than introducing ourselves to and talking with the stranger in the room?

Inaction is also prevalent when it comes to initiating Invite Welcome Connect in our communities of faith. Recently a priest approached me during a diocesan Invite Welcome Connect presentation, saying he now realized that he was the obstacle to this ministry getting off the ground at his church. Years back he had attended one of the Invite Welcome Connect workshops along with a group of parish leaders, but he never encouraged or helped implement the ideas they brought back. He had since repented of his inaction and was determined this time to return with enthusiasm for this ministry.

And sometimes our inaction is a result of indecision, of spinning our wheels. It's not for lack of interest; rather we get bogged down in what to do first or in the enormity of the work. For those facing this obstacle, I have two words: Get started. Make mistakes. Start down one path and then readjust your direction. Course correct as needed. But you can't change direction if you're still at the starting gate. Take the first steps. Get started. Otherwise, you will be in the same place tomorrow as today, and people who come to your churches for a taste of the heavenly banquet will leave hungry.

In the Diocese of Alabama, nearly a third of our ninety-two churches have participated in Invite Welcome Connect workshops. These churches range in size from 75 to 550 average Sunday attendance and are in locations from downtown and historic to suburban, from lake and resort to small town. After a year, these churches were polled about their successes and challenges while incorporating the Invite Welcome Connect ministry.

We found that when people are dedicated to implementing this ministry, they experience vibrancy and change in their congregation. In addition, we learned that there are as many ways to succeed in this ministry as there are people implementing it. What works for one church may fail at another. It is essential for you to know your church's personality to integrate this ministry into your church's way of being.

One of the most important things to remember is: Keep at it. Don't let one or two obstacles derail your ministry. Tweak your strategy when necessary. In the survey, some churches reported success with hosting a monthly Newcomer Cafe, and others failed miserably. One church revived its homemade bread ministry, and another tried to start one and floundered because of lack of leadership and participation from volunteers.

Start with things that are easy and don't require a large investment. Look for early success, then move to items that require funding.

Start with creating a team for each ministry area of Invite Welcome Connect, then empower and equip people to start (or stop) initiatives and programs. The key to success of this ministry is buy-in from the clergy and involvement and commitment of lay leaders.

Donna J. Gerold
Priest-in-Charge
Trinity Episcopal Church
Apalachicola, Florida

In addition to obstacles of complacency and inaction, we face "sacred cows" — traditions within the church that have become sacrosanct, almost idols within themselves. These include signage at our churches, the usher ministry, announcements, passing the peace during worship, etc.

Navigating the sacred cows in our churches while implementing Invite Welcome Connect can be particularly challenging, requiring the deft touch of wise clergy and lay leaders.

Navigating the sacred cows in our churches while implementing Invite Welcome Connect can be particularly challenging, requiring the deft touch of wise clergy and lay leaders. Early on in developing this ministry, I traveled to a small congregation in East Texas to lead a vestry retreat. As a part-time staff person gave me and the new rector a tour of the facilities, she commented that they had a problem with getting folks to come to coffee hour since the parish hall was separated from the nave by an outdoor courtyard. When I suggested they offer fellowship in the beautiful courtyard, she said they couldn't do that because of the bees. At the vestry retreat the next day, the rector asked me to tell the vestry about this encounter, and one of the men said he had attended this church his entire life and had never seen a bee on the property. The staff member apparently thought bees were attracted to donuts, hence she had become one of the unofficial gatekeepers of the coffee-hour tradition. I've told this story many times over the years. After one diocesan-wide presentation, the clergy of a large urban church remarked, "Those sacred cows you mention—we have a herd of them here!"

Addressing the sacred cows in our congregations takes a measured amount of grace, wisdom, and loving kindness as well as courageous leadership. Jimmy Abbott, rector of Holy Comforter Episcopal Church in Spring, Texas, talks about "the bad news—the hard edge of Invite Welcome Connect." In his plenary address at the 2016 Invite Welcome Connect Summit at Camp Allen in Texas, Jimmy noted that implementing this ministry sometimes reveals things in a parish that are not bearing fruit for God's kingdom, ministries you think are working but in fact are not. He shares the story of Holy Comforter's Labor Day barbeque, which the congregation had hosted for fourteen years with up to 500 folks in attendance. They considered it the "best thing since sliced bread," he said. It was a well-known community-wide event with a competitive cook-off. They made sure every utensil used at the barbeque contained information about their church and offered tours of the church during the event.

After utilizing some of the Invite Welcome Connect material, the leadership discerned that not a single person came to church as a result of the barbeque. Upon realizing that the barbeque was not bearing fruit for God's kingdom, the vestry made the hard decision to stop holding the event. Utilizing that great creative writing line, Jimmy exclaimed, "We killed our darling!" The church made the difficult choice to stop a beloved (and otherwise successful) tradition—a sacred cow. Other newer ministries at Holy Comforter were actually bearing fruit, bringing newcomers into the community and into relationship with Jesus, but congregation members were spending a great deal of energy on the barbeque, which was not fruitful in terms of newcomer ministry. Jimmy cautioned: "If you like your church exactly like it is and you think your church is perfect, then don't do Invite Welcome Connect because it'll mess you up! The good news [of implementing the ministry] is that people will show up, and the church has grown—we've doubled our size in four years!"

Jesus provides the model for how to confront our sacred cows. He fearlessly confronts tradition and institutions right and left. All four canonical gospels tell the story of Jesus expelling the money changers from the temple in Jerusalem and then returning later to critique the chief priests and other religious leaders. He challenges the customs of the day by engaging in conversation with the woman at the well and spending time with tax collectors. He does not tear down sacred cows simply for the sake of change but when these traditions become obstacles to relationships, Jesus always chooses love. Always.

In early 2001, Charles Deng, a Dinka refugee who had come to the United States a decade earlier, asked a dozen young Sudanese refugees whether they had been to church on their first Sunday in America. They said they had boarded a bus that came to their apartment complex and gone to a church. Yet as members of the Episcopal Church of Sudan, American church culture was foreign to them. Charles told them he knew where they should go to church. The next Sunday, he drove back and forth between their apartment complex and the Episcopal Church of the Ascension in Dallas, Texas, where they found a home. With Charles's intentional effort of invitation and connection, the people of the Church of the Ascension and the Sudanese community in Texas have been significantly, richly blessed.

The faithful one-on-one work of inviting and connecting those not yet part of the church requires intentional communal strategies if the congregation is to thrive as it joins God on a mission in the world. In particular, partnerships allow congregations to reach communities underrepresented in the congregation, such as those from different ethnicities, races, languages, or generations, and to experience and extend the health and transformation promised by the gospel.

Consider this metaphor. A church or faith community is a cell. An animal cell has internal structures designed to produce health and growth. A permeable cell membrane distinguishes that cell from another and allows the appropriate ingress and egress of fluids and chemicals, while slowing or delaying the introduction of dangerous substances. Though some substances pass freely through the membrane, others—even those required for health—bounce off if they do not encounter a receptor.

Though we like to imagine our faith communities as open to all, outsiders often experience us as closed and defended systems, if they are aware of and interested in our existence at all. When social factors intensify the separation, direct invitation of individuals or families rarely results in a noticeable shift in the demographics of the congregation. People from underrepresented cultures who find their way to a congregation often leave without true inclusion, even if they receive a well-intentioned welcome. This may spiritually impoverish those seeking a spiritual home and leaves the faith community without the relational capital to invest in extending its mission. Like a cell, a congregation needs receptors.

Receptors are those people in a church body who already have, or intentionally develop, relationships with outsiders connected to the communities with which the congregation hopes to be in relationship. These communities may be organizations with which the congregation shares common values, ethnic communities in need of solidarity with supportive friends, or persons facing an identifiable life challenge.

Most congregations already have potential receptors ready to facilitate connections through introductions and spadework. Clergy and lay leaders find them by becoming curious about things such as:

- Who in the congregation possesses the spiritual gifts of connecting and gathering?

- With whom, or with which groups, do their members already have relationships?

- Which groups of people are present in the city, town, or neighborhood but not in the congregation? How will you find out what their hopes, desires, and needs are? Imagine what you might have in common with their hopes, desires, and needs.

This first question identifies potential receptors. The second asks where receptors already exist. The third looks for opportunities for the congregation to identify and equip receptors.

The receptor and the connected outsider help initiate partnerships in which some members of the congregation meet and develop human connections with a community from which the congregation would otherwise be isolated. When church members enter those relationships with a spirit of curiosity and a willingness to serve alongside non-church members, all may discover opportunities to serve the common good together. As time passes, the receptors and congregation and their new friends may become ready to build Christian community together.

Kai Ryan
Canon to the Ordinary
The Episcopal Diocese of Texas

A recalibration of expectations is a challenge for some individuals. When we cast the net wide and become fishers of people as Jesus asks, our harvest will include all sorts of folks, not just those who look or act or talk like us. The whole body of Christ includes widows and young people, black and white, yellow and brown, single and married folks, rich and poor and all the in-betweens. Further, some people worry that implementation of the Invite Welcome Connect ministry will change what they currently value about their congregation.

I recently heard a vestry member of a small congregation articulate a common fear. She likes her church the size that it is (and by tacit omission, worries that she might not like it if the church grows). I wish I could allay this particular concern, but I can't. I believe that if we take seriously the ministry of Invite Welcome Connect, the composition of our congregations will change. And we will be better for it.

Several years ago, as part of my work for the Episcopal Church Foundation, I visited a small congregation on Sunday that had about twenty people in attendance. The sermon was fine, the music was lovely, and a glance at the program showed that they were doing good in the world. Later, during coffee hour, I chatted with the senior warden. He lamented how few people were interested in coming to the church and then casually uttered words I'll never forget: "The real problem is that there are so few Episcopalians in the neighborhood."

The neighborhood, it must be said, was one of the most densely populated, multicultural places in the nation. Even so, his invitation only extended to those who were already familiar with the rites and rhythms of the Episcopal Church. A very short invitation list, indeed.

While it's easy to caricature this particular exchange, I've had subtler versions of this conversation many times. When people say they want to invite people to church, there are oftentimes caveats to that statement.

- "We invite everyone...but especially people who can help us pay for a new roof."

- "We invite everyone...but we especially want parents with young children. Our congregation is so elderly."

- "We invite everyone...but especially people who can serve on the vestry or who are excited about the altar guild."

- "We invite everyone...but we especially want those who can appreciate our Anglican choral tradition."

Sometimes these caveats venture into darker territory. From a racist perspective, the Episcopal Church is growing in all the wrong places, with Latinos and Asian Americans being among the fastest growing segments of our church. From an elitist perspective, it's problematic that many of the growing segments of the church are fairly poor. As a denomination that is 90 percent white and has a deep, historical association with the nation's elite, extending an invitation to the growing diversity of our neighborhoods threatens to change our worship style, the language, the food, and the music of our communities of faith. And it's because of this that the invitation very often "gets lost in the mail."

We must not let the invitation get lost in the mail. Let us follow the Holy Spirit and allow this initial act of invitation to push us well beyond our comfort zones. Let us extend the invitation to those for whom terms like vestry, narthex, and sexton are entirely new terms, and who may, in the end, transform our way of understanding what it means to be church.

Miguel Escobar
Director of Anglican Studies
Episcopal Divinity School at Union Theological Seminary
New York City, New York

As I have taken the ministry of Invite Welcome Connect from coast to coast as well as to Canada and Europe, my hosts often warn me that their context, issues, and obstacles to this ministry are different from everyone else's. My mission—in my visits and in this book—is to acknowledge that despite our various obstacles, we humans are the same on the inside: We each have a need to be seen, heard, welcomed, and affirmed. The ministry of Invite Welcome Connect, if implemented prayerfully, intentionally, thoughtfully, and relationally, can meet these needs and desires. Boldness and courage are needed to face the challenges and obstacles head-on, giving new meaning to risk-taking for the sake of the gospel.

Benedictine nun Maria Boulding frames this notion of turning obstacle into opportunity in these words: "Obedience to God is a means of freeing us from our own limited expectations." In this ministry, there is a place for everyone—the introvert and extrovert, those comfortable greeting newcomers, those who work in the soup kitchen, and others who enjoy wrestling with difficult scripture in Bible study. We are simply called to be obedient to the God who gives us life, to discern our giftedness, and then to live into the authentic lives into which God calls us. As communities of faith, we are called to be beacons of light and safe havens of welcome.

PRAYER

Gracious God, we pray this day for our eyes and hearts to be opened to the obstacles that are holding us back from ministry. We ask you to take away the sin of complacency in our individual lives and in our communities of faith. We pray for wisdom and courage as we discern and confront the sacred cows in our midst, those inflexible and rigid ways that prevent us from doing creative ministry. We ask for boldness as we imagine, create, and envision the gospel truths of Invite Welcome Connect, turning obstacles into opportunities for the glory of God. *Amen.*

QUESTIONS FOR INDIVIDUALS

1. What are your personal obstacles to being fully engaged in ministry?

2. Ponder this quotation: *Obedience to God is a means of freeing us from our own limited expectations.* How do these words make you feel?

3. What are some specific, intentional things you can do to turn obstacles into opportunities?

QUESTIONS FOR GROUPS

1. Can you truthfully say your church is a friendly community or are you a community of friends?

2. Where can you identify complacency and inaction in your community of faith?

3. Can you identify the sacred cows in your midst? Do you have the courage to address them? What are some first steps in this work?

Chapter 7

TRANSFORMATION

Evangelism is not complete until the new person has become fully integrated into the Church and has become a disciple of Christ...Evangelism is not about recruitment but about transformation.

Claude E. Payne
Reclaiming the Great Commission

Transformation often happens in our lives when we are able to see old things in new ways, full of new possibilities. The primary vision for the ministry of Invite Welcome Connect is a hopeful one, with a vision and dream of transforming the culture of our beloved Episcopal Church from maintenance to mission. The Episcopal Church is where I and countless others have found love and acceptance, a place where God opened me up to wonder and love and where I have been able to use my God-given gifts and talents. The ministry of Invite Welcome Connect

gives people hope as they bear witness to the transformation of individual lives and congregations.

One of the Episcopal Church's gems is the Invite Welcome Connect ministry. This ministry's practical initiatives have transformed the way Good Shepherd Episcopal Church in Dallas, Texas, offers hospitality and connects with newcomers. And thanks to Mary Parmer's wisdom and guidance, our parish has become a place where newcomers are honored as guests and follow-up is intentional and authentic.

We launched Invite Welcome Connect in July 2014. Earlier that year, two clergy, a vestry member, and I attended the first conference. We became hooked on the clear and simple message of hospitality and returned to Dallas full of enthusiasm. Within weeks, we formed an Invite Welcome Connect team. Six months later, more than twenty parishioners attended an all-day Invite Welcome Connect session.

The essential of Welcome resonated with our group, and we agreed this was a great place to start. Mary reminded us that Jesus modeled welcome and hospitality wherever he went and that part of being a healthy church involved the practice of hospitality. Acknowledging that our newcomers' ministry needed improvement, we became deliberate about change.

Our Invite Welcome Connect team crafted a Welcome ministry training guided by the hallmark of Benedictine hospitality: "Let all guests who arrive be received as Christ." We encouraged our hospitality team (clergy, staff, greeters, and ushers) to reflect on Benedict's words and the distinctions between visitor and guest. A visitor comes and goes without much preparation on the part of a host or much thought afterward. A visitor attends museums, schools, and zoos, and personal follow-up from the host is not the norm. On the other hand, a guest is cared for and has been intentionally invited. Most of the time he/she is looking for a specific experience, and personal follow-up from the host is essential.

We started applying the "guest" model to our welcome practices. As these practices evolved, our Welcome focus shifted from smiles and waves in the pews to intentional, personal contact after the services. We started listening more and talking less. We established a newcomer follow-up system with personal touches from clergy, staff, and ministry leaders. Over a period of three months, we extended personal invitations to a special worship event, an outreach activity, and a fellowship opportunity. Weekly staff meetings included direct follow-up and connections assignments.

In the first year of implementing Invite Welcome Connect, we welcomed more than a hundred new members into our church family. And we have continued to see marked growth in membership and involvement. There's also been a renewed sense of belonging among our long-time members. They see change, and they're excited about it. Invite Welcome Connect has helped Good Shepherd become a place where all guests are welcomed as Christ.

Catherine Pryor Miller
Lay Leader
Good Shepherd Episcopal Church
Dallas, Texas

In the fall of 2015, I had the privilege of preaching at The General Theological Seminary in New York City, and my sermon centered on the feast day of Remigius, also known as Remi.

One of the patron saints of France, Remi was known for his learnedness and holiness of life, and at age 22, he was named a bishop. Remi was instrumental in the conversion and baptism of King Clovis of the Franks. And the king's conversion changed the course of religious history in Europe, as it led to the Franks' support of Pope Gregory the Great and his evangelistic efforts in England.

Just as one person's influence changed the course of history, so too can one person's influence transform an individual life. Sally Dooley's invitation to attend worship at her church sparked a transformation in my life that sent me on an entirely different trajectory. I am certain our churches are full of folks whose lives have been transformed and affected by one person's influence, and I hear these stories often as I travel around the country with the ministry of Invite Welcome Connect.

While at the seminary that fall, a student, John Shirley, shared with me his story of how Scott Bader-Saye, ethics professor at the Seminary of the Southwest, was influential in John becoming an Episcopalian. John's path had taken him to seminary and he was about to graduate and be ordained as an Episcopal priest. Where would John be today without the influence of Scott?

Using God's gift of creativity in ways that transform lives is at the core of the ministry of Invite Welcome Connect. I am privileged to hear and witness these stories of transformation that are occurring across our church, guided by the ministry of Invite Welcome Connect as people allow God to work in and through them. Clearly the Holy Spirit is at work.

Mary Parmer brought the ministry of Invite Welcome Connect to St. David's Church and School in January of 2014. We had renovated the sanctuary in 2013, and we were experiencing new life and new growth. St. David's has always been hospitable, but we needed a deeper and intentional awareness of who was in our community already and who was new. We wanted to learn how to communicate with words and actions that everyone mattered to the life of this church. It was time to take a mirror and hold it up to the life of our church and celebrate where we were healthy and to be honest about where we needed to change to make more room in our hearts for hospitality.

Mary had dinner with the vestry on Friday evening, asked a few leading questions, and then listened to our responses. On Saturday, we gathered with about ninety leaders in the congregation, and we dug deep and worked hard. With Mary's gift of helping us build a safe space to have the hard conversations and my encouragement to trust one another and be as objective as possible, we were ready to discover and learn more about our ministry of hospitality and connection. We discovered that people felt like certain aspects of our worship space did not match the energy of our people, so they were hesitant to invite others. We also learned that people wanted a new way to share information about who we are other than the newcomer Welcome bags. The woman who was largely responsible for creating those bags took a deep breath and said, "Thank goodness, I have thought those bags were tired for a long time." We then began the exciting exercise of envisioning what new things could take root in our ministry of Welcome.

Mary conveyed that this work required a healthy relationship with the staff so that these new ways of being were carried out together in the most effective way possible. Mary's whole way of being gives people permission to laugh, listen, share, and learn more about how God is calling us to be as the Body of Christ in our community. As the conversation continued, relationships deepened among us and a genuine excitement about being church was palpable.

As we began the worship services the following Sunday morning, I looked around and saw people on fire with a passion to open the doors and intentionally greet people, over and above giving them a bulletin. They made sure newcomers found a place to sit or helped them take their baby to the nursery and locate the restrooms. This time of hard work done in a loving and safe environment had an instant impact—and one that continues to this day. We review and update our online communications regularly and welcome feedback from the congregation and beyond. We are constantly scrutinizing and expanding or updating our written material as needed. Most importantly, the congregation now has a DNA of inviting, welcoming, and connecting people in a very natural and intentional way that is bringing life to the church and to the community around our campus.

Lisa Mason
Rector, St. David's Episcopal
Church and School
San Antonio, Texas

During the closing plenary session at the 2016 Invite Welcome Connect Summit, Jimmy Abbott of Holy Comforter Episcopal Church in Spring, Texas, shared how Invite Welcome Connect had changed him.

Invite Welcome Connect has changed my heart…It's not about getting somebody else to do something; it's about getting over our own vulnerabilities and proclaiming the gospel that we know…and in that process we become closer to the Lord Jesus. That's the real key to this, and I stand here to testify to the fact that this has changed my life, that I have come to know Jesus better by all of these things that Holy Comforter has done with Invite Welcome Connect. If you don't want to know Jesus more, then don't do this [Invite Welcome Connect]. But this is my invitation to you…that you try this, so you will come to know the Lord Jesus better.

> I have come to know Jesus better by all of these things that Holy Comforter has done with Invite Welcome Connect
>
> – Jimmy Abbott

These words speak to the core of Invite Welcome Connect. It is not a program to grow your church—though I'm convinced that your church will grow if you implement it. Invite Welcome Connect is not a panacea, a cure-all for the problems that ail either your particular congregation or post-modern Christianity—though I believe it's a good start for modeling and strengthening the Body of Christ. Invite Welcome Connect is a ministry focused on transformation, and that transformation begins first in the heart of an individual, and then another and another. This transformation occurs as people say yes to Jesus and yes to a deeper life of following him. Then the transformation moves out in circles, from family and friends to fellow church members, to neighbors and co-workers, to cities and towns, and beyond.

At St. John's in Tallahassee, Florida, Invite Welcome Connect offers a constant reminder for people to share their joy, to help others experience their own joy, and then in turn to share that joy with even more people. Recently we had a young mother join us with her three children. She was invited to our Invitation Sunday by a colleague and enjoyed the service. She came back and enrolled her children in Sunday school and came to our New Member Class. Afterward, she participated in our Growing in Grace class, preparation for adult confirmation. And at the Easter Vigil, she and her three children were baptized. They are a dynamic family who have truly found a home at St. John's.

During a turbulent time of transition, amidst a divorce and caring for three small children, this woman found a place to anchor her family and grow in faith and love. She also took the perspective, this ministry, one step further. She began the process over by sharing her joy with her cousins who live in town, inviting them to come to events with her, and then eventually inviting them to attend the New Member Class and be welcomed into the church family just like she has been. We are so thankful to see joy like this in our parish and her living example of sharing this joy with others.

Abigail W. Moon
Associate rector
St. John's Episcopal Church
Tallahassee, Florida

> *The way of Love, the way of Jesus, is a game changer, and to Invite Welcome Connect is to create space for God to do God's game-changing work!*
>
> *- Michael B. Curry*

At the close of his sermon at the first annual Invite Welcome Connect Summit in 2015, Bishop Michael B. Curry said this, "The way of Love, the way of Jesus, is a game changer, and to Invite Welcome Connect is to create space for God to do God's game-changing work!"

Across the country, congregational leaders are sharing stories of transformation through the ministry of Invite Welcome Connect. Luke Jernagan, rector of St. Peter's Church in Ladue, Missouri, a suburb of St. Louis, calls the changes in his congregation "nearly a miracle!"

Invite Welcome Connect has been transformational at St. Peter's. Since Mary's presentation in 2014, our average Sunday attendance has grown over 40 percent. But growth in membership and attendance has been the secondary effect. The primary transformation in our parish is the welcoming way that long-time parishioners treat each other. For the parishioners who took part in the Invite Welcome Connect work, considering the reasons why someone would join our parish has opened their eyes to the many ways God is present and working through this community. This has given folks a renewed zeal in inviting others to worship here. They're proud of their church! That sense of joy in sharing the gospel has become contagious, and it has been a blessing to watch. St. Peter's has become known in St. Louis as the joyful, welcoming church. Long-time parishioners would say that is nearly a miracle!

Implementing the ministry of Invite Welcome Connect requires courage. Clergy must be serious about leading the way in equipping people to share the gospel, and they must be unafraid to empower the laity for ministry. Likewise, lay leaders must be willing to step out of their comfort zones for the sake of the gospel, discerning their giftedness and using those gifts in the Body of Christ. We, both clergy and laity, need courage to confront the obstacles that are holding us back from ministry, and we need to use that courage to be more relational and intentional in everything we do. And we all must be willing to tap into our wondrous creativity so we might...

Imagine a church filled with members who are bursting with love for one another and God, who feel compelled to invite others to experience the same joy...

Imagine a church filled with people who have cultivated the ability to really see the other with the eyes of Jesus and truly welcome them...

Imagine a church filled with holy listeners, hearing the stories of those with whom we worship and those who have entered the doors of our churches for the first time...

Imagine a church filled with people who take the challenge of creativity seriously...

Imagine a church filled with courageous clergy and laity, with inspired risk-takers who see obstacle as opportunity...

Imagine a church transformed by a loving God.

I am convinced we can change the narrative and the culture of the Episcopal Church to move from maintenance to mission, from calling ourselves the "frozen chosen" to people who are energized and transformed, who worship and play and share our lives in dynamic communities of faith, places where God's life-changing love creates a safe space for the work of building up the kingdom of God.

Then, and only then, can we be witnesses for Jesus in the lives of those around us. We can be agents of change, displaying the glory of God and the love of God's people as part of the Episcopal branch of the Jesus Movement.

PRAYER

Dear gracious Lord, who has imbued each of us with the gifts of faith and hope, we ask you this day for the courage to be risk-takers for the sake of the gospel. May we be agents of imagination in our congregations, stretching our wings of faith and love and possibility. Help us to live faithfully into our calling as lay and ordained leaders, always seeing and welcoming the other. May we listen long and deeply to the stories of those with whom we worship, and may we model the ways of Jesus, love incarnate. *Amen.*

Appendix

The resources in this appendix provide support for those considering the Invite Welcome Connect ministry. They include a Getting Started guide, an example of how one congregation implemented this ministry, several checklists, and a resource list. But the appendix offers only a sampling of resources. Every community of faith can and should take these essentials and make them their own, meeting the needs of their particular context and location. The Invite Welcome Connect website features concrete action plans and ideas for each of the essentials — and the list is being updated and added to regularly.

Further, trained facilitators and coaches are available to assist congregations and dioceses in the structure and principles of the Invite Welcome Connect ministry. Visit www.invitewelcomeconnect.sewanee.edu to learn more.

GETTING STARTED

1. Schedule six one-hour sessions of your church leadership, including your clergy, leadership, newcomer, and evangelism teams.

2. Between sessions, ask participants to read the corresponding chapters. You can also encourage them to watch the videos for Invite Welcome Connect available on the website.

- Session one: Introduction and Chapter 1

- Session two: Chapter 2 Invite

- Session three: Chapter 3 Welcome

- Session four: Chapter 4 Connect

- Session five: Chapters 5-6: Creativity, Obstacles & Opportunities

- Session six: Chapter 7: Transformation&Implementation

3. Creative Idea Generation: After each discussion of the essentials, small groups of lay leaders and clergy seated around tables should generate ideas about invitation, hospitality, and connection. The rules for engaging this generative, creative process are:

- Let ideas flow generously

- Do not censor yourself—*i.e.,* begin asking how much time a certain idea will take, or what it will cost; let every idea live

- Give space for the voice of everyone at your respective tables

- Place each idea on a Post-it note

- Display Post-it ideas on windows, walls, or white easel paper

- Report ideas from each group

This brainstorming time sets aside space for beginning to reimagine the mission of your congregation. Ideas are generated by both clergy and laity, without prompting or approval of leadership. The success of Invite Welcome Connect depends a great deal on the support of congregational leaders. The flow of these workshops and their creative processes require a give and take that begins by engaging the voices and imagination of everyone in the room. This process represents the headwaters of creativity and initiative in congregations, enabling them to expand their presence to each other and to their neighborhoods. It's crucial for everyone to be involved.

Once you have collected your ideas, you can begin assessing which ones are most immediately and easily implemented and which ones will require more strategizing. But this process happens *after*, not before or within, the process of creative idea generation.

4. Continue the Creative Idea Generation during each of the first five sessions. During the sixth session, ask everyone to select which team they would like to join: Invite, Welcome, or Connect.

Take care to build teams with a balance of gender and age. Anyone can participate in this ministry. People who are energized by their faith and what God is doing in their lives might be good candidates for the Invite team. People with gifts of hospitality might feel particularly drawn to Welcome. And people who have deep listening skills and are passionate about helping people discern their gifts might be good Connect team members. Let people self-select (using their own spiritual gifts discernment as a tool) and then evaluate the teams for particular needs. Also, clergy are welcome on any of these teams, but the teams should be primarily composed of lay leaders.

5. Each team then takes ideas specific to their teams of Invite, Welcome, or Connect and builds a plan for implementation in their specific area.

6. Follow-up team meetings on a regular basis are encouraged.

7. At six months and then a year, measure the impact of the Invite Welcome Connect ministry. You may consider reconvening the original group to talk about what worked, what didn't, and next steps. Include newcomers in these conversations—they offer fresh eyes to the practices and traditions of the community.

IMPLEMENTATION

St. Thomas the Apostle Episcopal Church in Overland Park, Kansas, began its work with Invite Welcome Connect in 2014. This report by rector Gar Demo provides one church's example for building an infrastructure for the ministry and for implementation.

After about six months of discernment, St. Thomas launched an Invite Welcome Connect committee. The team meets approximately four times a year to review goals, check on progress, and set new vision for this work. The team includes the Invite Welcome Connect warden, usher coordinator, greeter coordinator, bread-baker coordinator, rector, parish administrator, assistant rector, children's minister, a vestry member, and two or three other lay members.

Here are various projects and goals since St. Thomas began the Invite Welcome Connect ministry that have been completed or are in process:

INVITE

- Started holding three invitation weekends per year. Prepared cards and other resources for members to invite neighbors and friends to worship or an activity. We have had some small success with this approach. We also made sure to add food to the reception time after services.

- We have made several videos for Facebook and Instagram along with advertisements for various holidays. Efforts have included invitation cards for members to give to others in the weeks before these holidays as well. We have had a noticeable increase in attendance by as much as 15 percent on Ash Wednesday, Christmas Eve, and Easter Sunday. Members are encouraged to check in to Saint Thomas on their social media channels for all activities they attend as a way of advertising (at no cost to us!).

- We have redesigned and reconfigured all external and internal signage to be more informative and welcoming to everyone who comes onto our campus.

WELCOME

- Appointed a Welcome coordinator who oversees our welcome materials and process.

- Reworked our Welcome bags for newcomers. Bags include freshly baked bread, information materials, custom pen (with light/stylus), pencils, mint, and magnet for refrigerator with service times, address, phone, website address, etc.

- Trained and recruited new ushers and greeters. All services, including special ones, have a full complement of ushers and greeters stationed around the church.

- Each greeter/usher has an identification badge that is clear and noticeable.

- Ushers welcome and guide people into worship. This includes junior ushers, children who are contributors in this ministry.

- Greeters look for new people and offer them welcome bags both before and after the services.

- Greeters and ushers encourage new people to fill out an information card but don't push too hard.

- Added welcome tables in two locations. Each table has name tags, basic information, newcomer cards, etc.

- Reworked existing Ministry Book, a catalog of the church's active ministries, so that it includes information on all aspects of St. Thomas and contact information for ministry leaders. This is reviewed quarterly and updated as often as possible.

- We are in the process of redesigning our narthex to house a new Welcome Center, which will serve as a more appealing and inviting space for newcomers to gather and for us to do the work of welcoming them into our community.

Once people are identified as newcomers, they move through the following steps within the first three months of attending St. Thomas:

- Receive a phone call from a lay member. During the phone call, newcomers are asked if they have any questions, invited back to services, told how to reach clergy, etc.

- Receive a handwritten note of welcome from the rector and a phone call after the second week of attendance

- If they continue to show interest in St. Thomas through attendance or giving to the church, we invite them to the next newcomer dinner. They are also sent a welcome kit prior to the dinner with more information and a membership form.

- The dinner is hosted by the rector and Invite Welcome Connect committee as well as three to five vestry members, some staff, and leaders of other ministries.

- Invite Welcome Connect chair follows up with staff and ministry leaders to make sure contact has been made.

CONNECT

- Examined all of our ministries to see how they connect with current members as well as new people joining St. Thomas. That work has included a ministry audit, some clarification of roles within the church, scheduling software (Ministry Scheduler Pro), and redesign of our website.

- Hosted connection fairs in the spring and fall of each year. One Sunday a month we host smaller connection fairs around a specific area of ministry, such as liturgy or outreach. We have held about twenty of these events.

- Met with ministry leaders and encouraged each group to consider periodic social events to build relationships. Examples: Adult youth group for parents of teens, Altar Guild spring and fall brunches, musician holiday party, etc.

- Began a monthly wine and food event for the Saturday Evening service. This once-a-month gathering is designed to help the congregation at that service feel more connected.

- Intentionally tracked members and their connections to at least one ministry. We now have 90 percent participation of members in at least one ministry. Within our newcomers, we have a 72 percent participation in at least one ministry.

- Re-emphasized name tags. We shifted from a name tag wall with pre-printed name tags to name tags that are stickers. With some effort, this has increased name tag usage—and doesn't exclude new members. Part of the challenge is that we don't have room now for a name tag wall with everyone's names!

- Started plans for a new pictorial directory.

- Restarted and emphasized dinners for groups. Each fall and spring, we invite people to sign up and attempt to connect with as many new people as possible. This has been one of the better successes in terms of deepening connection.

- Started seven new small groups, which gives us a total of eighteen active small groups.

- Offered Lenten Lunches, Advent classes, and new programs during the day and evening.

STATISTICS

Year	Average Sunday Attendance	Easter	Christmas	Members	Pledges
2014	277	690	685	768	205
2015	297	747	707	762	222
2016	310	784	746	826	228
2017	320	749	747	1057	232

Year	Baptism	Weddings	Funerals	Confirmations/ Received
2014	14	11	15	5
2015	13	8	23	28
2016	9	7	9	15
2017	8	5	21	18

INVITE:
ASSESSMENT

This checklist provides a starting place for you to assess your congregation's system for the Invite essential and to begin implementing a plan and structure for invitation. It is not intended to be either all-inclusive or size-specific. How you approach the Invite essential is based on the gifts of your congregation and the context of your community. Be honest in your answers and compare your initial responses to a follow-up assessment at six months and a year.

	We do this well	We need to work on this	We do not do this yet
We know how to talk about our faith			
We are comfortable inviting people to our church			
We can answer the questions: Why do you believe in God? How has faith in Christ changed your life?			
Physical tools for invitation are provided to members i.e., business cards, postcards, etc.			
Education & training classes and/or teaching resources are provided to help parishioners learn how to effectively evangelize, i.e. how to share their faith story, how to invite someone to church			
Our church offers numerous creative ways of invitation to the local community, intentionally connecting these activities with information about our church			

We do this well	We need to work on this	We do not do this yet	
			Do we know our church's neighbors? Do they know us?
			Demographics, opportunities, and needs of the neighborhoods around our church are clearly defined and known
			Our church partners with outside groups in outreach efforts
			Our clergy, staff, and lay leadership are affiliated with local civic and community groups, i.e., Rotary Club, Chamber of Commerce, Lions Club, Kiwanis, etc.
			Our clergy, staff, and/or leadership have cultivated relationships with local media, e.g. local newspaper, radio, TV station
			Our church experiments with creative advertising efforts
			Our website is up-to-date, relevant, and understandable for newcomers
			Our newsletter is up-to-date, relevant, and can be easily accessed online
			We use social media in creative ways as an evangelism tool
			Our membership contact information is up-to-date and includes email and physical addresses

WELCOME: ASSESSMENT

This checklist provides a starting place for you to assess your congregation's system for the Welcome essential and to begin implementing a plan and structure for hospitality. It is not intended to be either all-inclusive or size-specific. How you approach the Welcome essential is based on the gifts of your congregation and the context of your community. Be honest in your answers and compare your initial responses to a follow-up assessment at six months and a year.

	We do this well	We need to work on this	We do not do this yet
The church voicemail uses a warm, friendly greeting that offers current information about service days and times, and instructions (or an emergency number) for leaving messages for staff			
Road signage and/or banners contain information that is easy to read from a moving vehicle			
All indoor and outdoor facilities are clean, inviting, attractive, clearly tended and cared for			
Nursery is accessible, clean, attractive to adults and children and meets all requirements of the diocese and state for lawful operation			
Interior signage includes clearly marked entryways, walkways, and map of facilities			
Restrooms are well marked, clean, and have plenty of supplies on hand			
Designated guest parking is near the front doors and clearly identifiable			

We do this well	We need to work on this	We do not do this yet	
			We have a robust greeting and welcome team
			Greeters are stationed at the parking lot, narthex, welcome table, and entrance doors
			Phone calls and emails are responded to promptly
			Ushers are stationed at the narthex, entrance into nave
			An information/welcome center is clearly identified and staffed with friendly greeters
			Name tags: Either everyone wears them—or no one does
			Clergy are available at the door of the church before and/or after worship
			Clergy offer words of welcome before or during service
			A system is in place for identifying guests/visitor/newcomers
			Welcome gift and/or information packet for newcomers is standard policy
			Activity bags are standard policy as a sign that we welcome children
			Worship bulletin is accessible, newcomer friendly; understandable to someone who has never been to church

	We do this well	We need to work on this	We do not do this yet
We explain insider language (EYC, ECW) and use as teachable moments			
We have accessible resources (handouts, pamphlets, etc.) that explain the Episcopal Church and answer other standard newcomer questions			
Announcements are inviting, with people introducing themselves and explaining events or ministries			
Hospitality time (coffee hour) after worship is easily accessible to newcomers			
We pay intentional attention to visitors/guests/newcomers during coffee hour			
Newcomers receive a phone call, text, or email from clergy following first visit			
Newcomers receive a phone call, text, or email within first week from lay leader(s)			
Welcome gift is delivered within the first three days, if not given at time of visit			
Newcomers receive handwritten note, preferably from clergy, within first week after visit			
We have a system in place to identify newcomers			

We do this well	We need to work on this	We do not do this yet	
			We provide ongoing training for Welcome team, including greeters, ushers, hospitality team
			Clergy/staff/leadership routinely evaluate Welcome ministry
			We occasionally invite others to be "mystery worshipers" to offer a fresh-eyed assessment of our community

CONNECT: ASSESSMENT

This checklist provides a starting place for you to assess your congregation's system for the Connect essential and to begin implementing a plan and structure for help people feel like they belong. It is not intended to be either all-inclusive or size-specific. How you approach the Connect essential is based on the gifts of your congregation and the context of your community. Be honest in your answers and compare your initial responses to a follow-up assessment at six months and a year.

	We do this well	We need to work on this	We do not do this yet
We have a tracking system in place to shepherd newcomers			
We have intentional conversations with each newcomer			
We connect newcomers with people and ministries that match their particular life phase, gifts, talents, passion			
We have written descriptions of each ministry and contact information available on website and in booklet form for distribution to newcomers			
We offer listening skills training on a regular basis			
We offer a newcomer orientation/new member class			
We offer classes for rites of initiation: baptism, confirmation, reception			

We do this well	We need to work on this	We do not do this yet	
			We offer many opportunities for spiritual nurture/discipleship
			Laity are empowered for ministry
			We help people claim their life's work as ministry and talk about spiritual practices and discerning gifts, strengths, and vocation
			We have regular meetings with the leadership of our ministries
			Each lay ministry functions as a small group, offering encouragement and pastoral care to group members
			We communicate about the various ministries through newsletters, websites, Facebook, ministry booklets, worship bulletins, and other sources
			We recognize, affirm, and celebrate the work of lay leaders and lay-led ministries
			We have entrance conversations with people who join our church, asking them questions that could help shape our ministry
			We have exit conversations with people who leave our church, asking them questions that could help shape our ministry

RESOURCES

These resources are cited in this book. For additional resources, visit the Invite Welcome Connect website at www.invitewelcomeconnect. sewanee.edu.

INTRODUCTION AND CHAPTER 1

My Mississippi, Willie Morris (University Press of Mississippi, 2000)

The Artist's Way, Julia Cameron (G. P. Putnam's Sons, 1992)

Culture Making, Andy Crouch (IVP Books, 2013)

Reclaiming the Great Commission, Claude E. Payne & Hamilton Beazley (Jossey-Bass, 2000)

Mindset: The New Psychology of Success, Carol S. Dweck (Ballantine Books, 2007)

Brightest and Best: A Companion to the Lesser Feasts and Fasts, Sam Portaro (Cowley Publications, 1998)

CHAPTER 2 - INVITE

Transforming Evangelism, David Gortner (Church Publishing, 2008)

Mere Christianity, C. S. Lewis (Macmillan, 1952)

Telling Secrets, Frederick Buechner (HarperOne, 2000)

CHAPTER 3 – WELCOME

Beyond Words, Frederick Buechner (HarperOne, 2004)

The Rule of Benedict: Insights for the Ages, Joan Chittister (Crossroad Publishing, 1992)

Love Walked Among Us: Learning to Love like Jesus, Paul Miller (NavPress, 2014)

An Altar in the World: A Geography of Faith, Barbara Brown Taylor (HarperOne, 2010)

CHAPTER 4 – CONNECT

Life Together, Dietrich Bonhoeffer (HarperOne, 2009)

The Crucifixion, Fleming Rutledge (Eerdmans, 2015)

The Power of Listening: Building Skills for Mission and Ministry, Lynne Baab (Rowman & Littlefield Publishers, 2014)

A Spirituality of Listening: Living What We Hear, Keith Anderson (IVP Books, 2016)

Falling Upward, Richard Rohr (Jossey-Bass, 2011)

Wellesley Centers for Women: https://www.wcwonline.org/2010/humans-are-hardwired-for-connection-neurobiology-101-for-parents-educators-practitioners-and-the-general-public

APPENDIX

CHAPTER 5 – CREATIVITY

The Preaching Life, Barbara Brown Taylor (Cowley Publications, 1993)

The Screwtape Letters, C. S. Lewis (HarperOne, 2015)

The Soul of the Congregation: An Invitation to Congregational Reflection, Thomas Edward Frank (Abingdon Press, 2000)

Christianity for the Rest of Us, Diana Butler Bass (HarperOne, 2007)

Holy Curiosity: Cultivating the Creative Spirit in Everyday Life, Amy Hollingsworth (Wipf & Stock Pub, 2011)

Beauty: The Invisible Embrace, John O'Donohue (Harper Perennial, 2005)

Daring Greatly: How the Courage to be Vulnerable Transforms the Way We Live, Love, Parent, and Lead, Brené Brown (Avery, 2015)

Acknowledgments

First, I would like to thank Sally Dooley and Don Joseph for inviting me to attend church with them twenty-three years ago and for being gracious embodiments of the Invite essential of this ministry. I am grateful for Patrick and Kay Gahan and the St. Stephen's Beaumont, Texas, family of faith for welcoming me into their hearts and lives. I am grateful to Bishop Claude E. Payne for inviting me to work for the Gathering of Leaders and especially his enthusiastic endorsement of this ministry.

I am thankful for Mary MacGregor and Bishop Andy Doyle for inviting me to further develop the St. Stephen's newcomer process. I am grateful for Carol Barnwell's creative ideas in the development stages of this ministry, and I appreciate Julie Heath's diligent administrative work for the national Invite Welcome Connect summits held at Camp Allen. I'm thankful for Lucy Strandlund's work as my research assistant for toolkit ideas for Invite Welcome Connect and for blessed encouragement from De Sellers, Belton Zeigler, Kathleen Boudreaux, and my Benedictine brothers Michael and Peter. I appreciate Frank Allen's initial invitation to bring the ministry ouside of Texas and the countless Episcopalians who attended trainings in the early years of developing this ministry, sharing their insights and ideas for improving the newcomer process.

I am particularly grateful to Bishop Duncan Gray for suggesting I check out the Beecken Center as a home for Invite Welcome Connect, and I am thankful for Dean J. Neil Alexander, Courtney Cowart, and Jim Goodmann for enthusiastically welcoming me to Sewanee. Jim has been especially helpful during this transition, serving as a listening ear and first reader of the manuscript.

I am immensely grateful to my Invite Welcome Connect Advisory Team as they help me strategize and implement the vision for this ministry: Donna Gerold, Chris Harris, Matt Holcombe, Mary MacGregor, Lisa Mason, Catherine Pryor Miller, Brent Owens, Paul Pradat, Hillary D. Raining, David Romanik, and Jim Smalley.

I am thankful for Presiding Bishop Michael B. Curry's endorsement and enthusiasm for the ministry of Invite Welcome Connect, and I am grateful for his willingness to write the foreword.

I am indebted to the amazing generous contributors in this book: Jimmy Abbott, J. Neil Alexander, G. Brooks Butler, Molly Wills Carnes, Tom Dahlman, Gar Demo, Miguel Escobar, Hal Foss, Patrick Gahan, Donna J. Gerold, Christian Hawley, Tom Hotchkiss, Luke Jernagan, David C. Killeen, Lisa Mason, Richard McKeon, Catherine Pryor Miller, Abigail W. Moon, John Ohmer, Brent Owens, Jamie L. Pahl Jr., Paul Pradat,

ACKNOWLEDGMENTS

Hillary D. Raining, Jason T. Roberts, Mary Lee Robertson, Kai Ryan, Susan Brown Snook, Stephanie Spellers, and Jered Weber-Johnson.

I am grateful to Scott Gunn of Forward Movement for encouraging me through the years to write a book about this ministry. I am deeply indebted to Richelle Thompson for being an amazing editor, encouraging me, lifting me up when I was down, and gently pushing me to meet the deadlines.

I am grateful for my Southern Baptist family of origin, especially my sisters Ann and Nan, who nursed me during recovery from surgery and put up with my angst as I tried to meet my deadlines. I give thanks to God every day for my heavenly cheerleaders, Weir, Ibby, Debby, and my parents, Ike and Louise. I am deeply grateful to my family, Jason and Leigh, Lauren and Anthony, Jay, Keaton, Braeden, Abi, Ike, and Jedidiah, as I've taken time away from them in the last seven years to work two jobs and birth this "baby" named Invite Welcome Connect!

About the Author

Mary Foster Parmer is director of Invite Welcome Connect at the Beecken Center in the School of Theology of the University of the South in Sewanee, Tennessee. She is past director of the Gathering of Leaders, a national leadership gathering of young Episcopal clergy. Parmer has served as lay deputy to the past four General Conventions of the Episcopal Church, and she currently serves on the Task Force on Clergy Leadership Formation in Small Churches. Parmer holds a degree in religious studies from St. Edward's University in Austin, Texas, and formerly served as director of adult ministries & evangelism at St. Stephen's, Beaumont. Parmer has two married children and six young grandchildren and spends her time away from the office hiking, building stone labyrinths, and reading memoirs.

About the Contributors

JIMMY ABBOTT is the rector of Holy Comforter Episcopal Church in Spring, Texas. Since his call in 2012, the congregation has doubled in size, launched five missional communities in the surrounding neighborhood, and broken ground on construction for a new worship space. He graduated from the University of Texas in 2006 with a degree in history and from the Virginia Theological Seminary in 2010, where he wrote his thesis, "A Loud and Ungrounded Noise: The Antiwar Movement in the Episcopal Church during the Vietnam War." His wife, Maggie, is a physical therapist who cares primarily for the elderly and those with Parkinson's Disease.

J. NEIL ALEXANDER is the dean, professor of liturgy, and Charles Todd Quintard Professor of Theology in the School of Theology of the University of the South, Sewanee, Tennessee, the home of Invite Welcome Connect. He previously served as the diocesan bishop of the Episcopal Diocese of Atlanta and has taught at Wilfrid Laurier, Yale, Drew, and Emory universities, at The General Theological Seminary, and previously at Sewanee.

G. BROOKS BUTLER is a parishioner at St. John's Episcopal Church in Tallahassee, Florida. He has been an active member of the St. John's congregation since joining in 2015 and has been involved with the Invite Welcome Connect ministry since it was formed in 2016. He currently serves as the chair of the Invite Welcome Connect ministry at St. John's. Outside of St. John's Episcopal Church, Brooks works as an environmental engineer and is an active member of the Tallahassee community.

MOLLY WILLS CARNES left a twenty-five-year corporate career in 2014, discerned a call to lay ministry, and now considers herself a "spiritual bartender." Her ministry is marked by a deep empathy for those wounded by their church experience as she helps seekers across the United States return to Christian community. Carnes led an evangelism ministry at St. Mary's Episcopal Church in Cypress, Texas, guided by a passionate commitment to the baptismal covenant and the great commission. She convenes a monthly gathering of welcome leaders in the Houston area and is a certified facilitator for Invite Welcome Connect. Wife, mother, actor, writer, and activist are other roles she claims with joy.

MICHAEL BRUCE CURRY is the twenty-seventh presiding bishop and primate of the Episcopal Church. He is the chief pastor and serves as president and chief executive officer and chair of the Executive Council of the Episcopal Church. Throughout his ministry, Curry has been active in issues of social justice, reconciliation, immigration policy, and marriage equality. Curry has served on the boards of a large number of organizations, including as chair and now honorary chair of Episcopal Relief & Development. Curry has a national preaching and teaching ministry, having been featured on *The Protestant Hour* and as a frequent speaker at conferences around the country. He has written three books: *Following the Way of Jesus: Church's Teachings in a Changing World*; *Songs My Grandma Sang*; and *Crazy Christians: A Call to Follow Jesus*. He was one of the subjects of *In Conversation: Michael Curry and Barbara Harris* by Fredrica Harris Thompsett and is well-known as the preacher for the royal wedding of the Duke and Duchess of Sussex.

Tom Dahlman serves as the rector of Emmanuel Episcopal Church in Shawnee, Oklahoma. He is also a co-host of the podcast "Fundamentally Drained" with Everett Lees and Justin Dixon. He studied at the Seminary of the Southwest in Austin, Texas, graduating in 2015 with a master of divinity degree. He also has a master's degree in ministry from Oklahoma Christian University in Edmond. Prior to becoming an Episcopalian, Dahlman was a minister in the Churches of Christ for ten years, working as an associate and a youth and family minister. Dahlman gets very excited about good coffee, authentic Mexican food, a round of golf, the fact that his Volvo Wagon has 226,000 miles, Belgian beer, and great theology or history books, but he is especially thrilled when he has the chance to share with the unchurched and burned-out Evangelicals the treasure he has found in the Episcopal Church and the Anglican Communion.

Gar Demo serves as rector of St. Thomas the Apostle Episcopal Church in Overland Park, Kansas. He is passionate about welcoming and connecting people into a relationship with Jesus Christ. He has helped to develop a ministry called Thom's Helpers that seeks to welcome those with special needs into membership and ministry within the church. He has served widely in leadership roles in several dioceses. Demo attended the Episcopal Theological Seminary of the Southwest (ETSS) in

Austin, Texas, after receiving his bachelor's degree in psychology with a minor in music from Wichita State University. He was ordained to the priesthood in 1997. He also earned a master of business administration from Friends University in 2010.

MIGUEL ESCOBAR is director of Anglican studies at Episcopal Divinity School at Union Theological Seminary (EDS at Union). Until recently, he served as managing director of leadership and external affairs at the Episcopal Church Foundation and prior to that was communications assistant to the Most Rev. Katharine Jefferts Schori. He received his master of divinity degree in 2007 from Union Theological Seminary, is a member of Grace Church Brooklyn Heights, and lives in Brooklyn, New York.

HAL FOSS serves as treasurer of the Memorial Church of the Good Shepherd in Parkersburg, West Virginia. He is a lifelong Episcopalian. He graduated from Davidson College with a degree in chemistry and Columbia University with a master's degree in chemical engineering. After working for thirty-five years in the chemical industry, he is now retired. He has been active in Faith Alive for several years and has led Faith Alive weekends in ten states.

PATRICK GAHAN has been married to his childhood sweetheart, Kay, for forty-two years. They have three grown children, three grandchildren, and two more on the way. Gahan has served as an infantry officer in the U.S. Army and as a teacher and coach in both public and private schools. Most of his thirty years in the ordained ministry have been in the dioceses of Texas and West Texas, but he has served in Maryland, Tennessee, and

Newfoundland as well. For the past six years, Gahan has been rector of Christ Episcopal Church in San Antonio, Texas.

DONNA J. GEROLD is an Episcopal priest who has recently accepted a call as priest-in-charge at Trinity Church in Apalachicola, Florida, a historic church on Florida's Forgotten Coast. After graduating from the Seminary of the Southwest in Austin, Texas, in 2013, she returned to her home diocese of Alabama to serve as associate rector at St. Stephen's Episcopal Church, Birmingham, with a focus on outreach, adult formation, and evangelism. Outside of church, she loves gardening, long walks, reading, and pottery.

CHRISTIAN HAWLEY is a priest at St. Matthew's Episcopal Church Austin, Texas. He and his wife, Madeline (also a priest), spend a lot of time on the trails of Texas connecting with one another, the Holy Spirit, parishioners, veterans, and creatures great and small.

THOMAS S. "TOM" HOTCHKISS is an Episcopal priest in Dallas, Texas, where he serves as vicar on the staff of Good Shepherd Church & School. Hotchkiss is a graduate of Vanderbilt University, Fuller Theological, and Virginia Theological Seminary. Hotchkiss loves God and loves people. He is married to Marcia, and they have two adult sons, a daughter-in-law, and an amazingly energetic rescued terrier named Roma. From parishes in Tennessee, Alabama, and Texas and for close to thirty-five years of full-time ministry, Hotchkiss has been involved in inviting, welcoming, and connecting people in their faith and in the church.

LUKE JERNAGAN is rector of St. Peter's Church in Ladue, Missouri, a suburb of St. Louis. He is passionate about evangelism, preaching, teaching, and bringing new and cradle parishioners closer to God and enriching their passion for the Christian faith. Luke is married to Hopie, also an Episcopal priest, and they have three children. He graduated from the University of Alabama in 2003 and received his master of divinity and master of sacred theology degrees from The General Theological Seminary in 2006 and 2008.

DAVID C. KILLEEN serves as rector of St. John's Episcopal Church, Tallahassee, Florida. His ministry focuses on preaching and teaching, interfaith and ecumenical partnerships, and local and global outreach. Prior to St. John's, Killeen served for three years as associate rector of St. Mark's Episcopal Church in Jacksonville, Florida, and as curate and interim priest at St. Mary's, Tuxedo Park, New York. He is an honors graduate of The General Seminary of the Episcopal Church and Muhlenberg College. He and his wife, Carol, are the parents of four sons.

LISA MASON is the rector of St. David's Episcopal Church and School. She is a graduate of Southern Methodist Univerity, was in the real estate business for twenty-three years, and earned a master of divinity degree from the Seminary of the Southwest in Austin, Texas. She has been on the Board of Trustees of the Seminary of the Southwest since 2009. She loves serving a church that has a school as well as the opportunity to serve in many areas of diocesan life such as development, camps and conference ministry, and the Episcopal Schools Commission. She is passionate about being the church in the world, being open and welcoming, and believing that people are hungry to know they are loved, they matter, and they can make a difference.

St. David's is active in many ministries in the surrounding community and beyond, including feeding ministries, mission work, and opening their doors to community groups. Mason is married to Kirk, and they have two grown sons, Rand and John, daughter-in-law, Rachael, and Andrei, an adopted grown son from Belarus. Mason enjoys time with family, being outdoors hiking, swimming, gardening, playing with their new puppy, and loving life!

RICHARD MCKEON has been rector of the Episcopal Church of the Messiah in Rhinebeck, New York, since August 2010. He attended the College of the Resurrection in Mirfield, West Yorkshire, England, and finished his seminary education at Yale Divinity School, graduating in 1985. His interests include gardening, reading, and architecture, having written an undergraduate thesis on the architecture of Richard Morris Hunt and the use of house imagery in the novels of Henry James and F. Scott Fitzgerald. His graduate thesis was on the architecture of the Cathedral of St. John the Divine and its relationship to the contemporary culture of America. He currently serves as president of the board of the Friends of Clermont, is a trustee of the Cathedral of St. John the Divine, and is passionate about the preservation of the beauty of the Hudson Valley. McKeon continues to use the tools of Invite Welcome Connect to deepen his parish ministry. He currently lives in Clermont, New York, with his partner, Tim Lewis.

Ministry is in CATHERINE PRYOR MILLER's blood. A former missionary kid, she's passionate about helping people find God in their everyday lives. She's a spiritual director and retreat leader and serves on the Advisory Board of Invite Welcome Connect. In the last ten years, she's held leadership positions on her home church's vestry and steering committees for youth and pastoral programs. She also spent more than four years serving as director of pastoral programs and adult formation at Good Shepherd Episcopal Church in Dallas, Texas, where she was instrumental in the launch and implementation of Invite Welcome Connect. Miller and her husband, Matt, recently celebrated twenty-eight years of marriage, and their pride and joy are two young adult children, Caroline and Pryor. Miller is a contemplative yoga practitioner, and lover of travel, animals, special-needs kids, and all things related to Christian spirituality.

ABIGAIL W. MOON serves as associate rector at St. John's Episcopal Church, Tallahassee, Florida. Her ministry focuses on working with leadership teams on Christian formation of all ages and outreach locally and globally. She is a 2011 graduate of The School of Theology, in Sewanee, Tennessee. Prior to seminary, she worked in youth ministry at Church of the Good Shepherd in Augusta, Georgia, and Church of the Advent in Spartanburg, South Carolina. After college she served as a Peace Corps volunteer in Guinea, West Africa, and worked as a teacher.

JOHN OHMER has more than twenty years of experience as a parish priest in the Episcopal Church. He joined The Falls Church Episcopal as rector in September 2012 after having led the vibrant congregation of St. James' Episcopal Church in Leesburg, Virginia, for thirteen years. He is a graduate of Wabash College and earned a master of divinity from Virginia Theological Seminary. Prior to ordination, he had a brief career in government and politics, working as a Capitol Hill staff member and as a press secretary and speech writer in his home state of Indiana. Ohmer and his wife, Mary, an elementary school teacher, have three children. Ohmer blogs at Unapologetic Theology, unapologetictheology.blogspot.com.

After fifteen years as a trial attorney in Florida, BRENT A. OWENS answered the call to ordained ministry and graduated from the Seminary of the Southwest in Austin, Texas, in 2005. Owens is the associate dean of Christ Church Cathedral, Lexington, Kentucky, and is a strong believer in both prayer and action. He seeks to help empower the congregation he has been called to serve so that together they can carry out God's dream for the world. Owens and his wife, Malinda, have been married for thirty-two years, have three children, and just became grandparents. Owens enjoys cycling and restoring and driving old British sports cars.

JAMES L. PAHL JR. received a bachelor of arts degree from North Carolina State University in 1995 and attended Virginia Theological Seminary, receiving his master of divinity degree in 2005 and his doctor of ministry in 2018. As an Episcopal priest, he served as assistant rector at St. James Episcopal Church in Wilmington, North Carolina beginning in 2005. In 2008, Pahl became the rector of St. Stephen's Episcopal Church in Oxford, North Carolina. He serves on several community and diocesan boards that focus on the faith community, government, and local stakeholders partnering together to address socioeconomic issues. Pahl is a singer/songwriter on the side, loves spending time in the mountains, and recently completed a life-changing pilgrimage to the Holy Land. He and his wife, Susie, are the parents of four children.

PAUL PRADAT is currently the rector of St. Thomas Episcopal Church in Huntsville, Alabama. The son of an Episcopal priest, Pradat was ordained to the priesthood in 1989. He has served congregations in the dioceses of Alabama and Mississippi. In addition, his personal journey has led him to work in the addiction treatment field. Pradat was the chief clinical officer at Cumberland Heights in Nashville, Tennessee when he accepted an offer to return to the Diocese of Alabama. As a lifelong Episcopalian, Pradat has always viewed the concepts contained in the Invite Welcome Connect ministry as a challenge but also an extraordinary opportunity for the church.

HILLARY D. RAINING is an Episcopal priest, author, wife and mother, yoga instructor, and beekeeper. She serves as the rector of St. Christopher's Episcopal Church in Gladwyne, Pennsylvania. She holds a bachelor's degree with honors in religion and psychology from Moravian College and a master of divinity from Yale and the Institute of Sacred Music, and is a graduate of Drew University with a doctorate in ministry. In addition to her educational background, she plays piano, classical violin, and Celtic fiddle. Raining serves on several diocesan and church-wide committees. She is the author of two books, *Joy in Confession* and *Faith with a Twist*, both with Forward Movement.

JASON T. ROBERTS is the rector of the Episcopal Church of the Holy Spirit in San Antonio, Texas. Beginning as the congregation's vicar in 2009, Roberts has journeyed with the Holy Spirit congregation through the sale of land, gathering in a temporary worship space, purchase of land, the joining together of two congregations, construction of a Sacred Space, the adopting of a twenty-eight-year-old preschool, a renewed focus on local outreach relationships, retreats, Bible studies, and the development of a more culturally rich congregation. In 2015, the congregation moved from mission to parish status. Every day Roberts and the Holy Spirit congregation learn more about how to invite, welcome, and connect with one another and anyone willing to share in the learning, living, and telling of Christ's story.

MARY LEE ROBERTSON, a retired educator of thirty-six years, is the mother of five and the grandmother of thirteen. Robertson has been an Episcopalian since her baptism in 1940 at St. John's Episcopal Church, Tallahassee, Florida. She was honored and blessed to be asked by her priest to serve as the chair of Invite Welcome Connect, helping to give birth to this important ministry at St. John's. She continues to be a member of the Connect and the Welcome teams. Robertson is passionate in her conviction that no one should be a stranger in our midst. Her belief that every person has a unique gift to offer comes not only from her many years of working with youth but also from her sincere love of people. Being involved in the Invite Welcome Connect ministry and other outreach ministries enriches her life in Christ.

KAI RYAN came out of the delivery room at the Miners' Hospital in Raton, New Mexico, and into the font at Holy Trinity Episcopal Church. Life in the church reveals the rhythms of God's grace and guidance for Ryan. The youngest of four sisters, she attended public schools in Albuquerque. Enjoying athletics, she competed in gymnastics, track, and cross country. Her life in Christ and leadership gifts were nurtured in camping ministry, the Happening movement, and parish committees, including one that resettled a refugee family. On receiving a bachelor's degree at the University of the South in Sewanee, Tennessee, Ryan returned to Albuquerque to gain employment experience required before seeking ordination. She married Tim Ryan in 1989, and they have two children, Ned and Eleanor. After receiving a master of divinity degree from the Seminary of the Southwest in Austin, Texas, Ryan spent twenty years in parish ministry, including fourteen years as rector of Ascension Episcopal Church in Dallas. There, she learned from brothers and sisters of other cultures how to lead a multi-ethnic community. Since 2014, Ryan has served as canon to the ordinary of the Diocese of Texas, leading the ministry staff in its work to implement the diocesan vision.

SUSAN BROWN SNOOK serves as canon to the ordinary for church growth and development in the Episcopal Diocese of Oklahoma, leading ministries of congregational development, evangelism, church planting, and spiritual and numerical growth. She also leads a staff team that includes communications, Christian formation, and stewardship. Previously, she was church planter, vicar, and then rector of the Episcopal Church of the Nativity in Scottsdale, Arizona, from 2006 to 2017. Snook received her master of divinity degree from Church Divinity School of the Pacific in 2003 and is currently working toward a doctor of ministry degree from Virginia Theological Seminary. She is a co-editor of *Acts to Action: The New Testament's Guide to Evangelism and Mission* and is a founder and leader of the Acts 8 Movement. She and her husband, Tom, have two amazing daughters.

STEPHANIE SPELLERS serves as the presiding bishop's canon for evangelism, reconciliation, and creation care and is the author of several books, including *Radical Welcome. She* has led renewal efforts across the Episcopal Church, co-chaired the Standing Commission on Mission and Evangelism, taught at The General Theological Seminary, and founded The Crossing community at St. Paul's Cathedral in Boston. She is former chaplain to the House of Bishops and lives in New York City.

JERED WEBER-JOHNSON is a husband, father of two young boys, Episcopal priest, and food enthusiast. He has been rector of St. John the Evangelist in Saint Paul, Minnesota since 2011. At Saint John's, Weber-Johnson's ministry has centered on Christian discipleship, congregational growth and development, and helping the faith community clarify its mission in and with the surrounding neighborhood. In recent years, St. John's has launched Invite Welcome Connect ministry, partnered with a local Hmong majority Episcopal Church in the creation of a farmer's market in the church parking lot, and developed a growing weekly Compline liturgy that primarily reaches young professionals and empty-nesters in the neighborhood. Prior to coming to St. John's, Weber-Johnson was assistant rector at St. Alban's in Washington, D.C., and grants officer at Trinity Grants in New York City. He holds a master of divinity degree from The General Theological Seminary in New York and a bachelor's degree from Greenville College in Greenville, Illinois.

About Forward Movement

Forward Movement is committed to inspiring disciples and empowering evangelists. We live out our ministry by creating resources such as books, small-group studies, apps, and conferences. Our daily devotional, *Forward Day by Day*, is also available in Spanish (*Adelante Día a Día*) and Braille, online, as a podcast, and as an app for smartphones or tablets. It is mailed to more than fifty countries, and we donate nearly 30,000 copies each quarter to prisons, hospitals, and nursing homes.

We actively seek partners across the church and look for ways to provide resources that inspire and challenge. A ministry of the Episcopal Church for over eighty years, Forward Movement is a nonprofit organization funded by sales of resources and by gifts from generous donors.

To learn more about Forward Movement and our resources, visit www.ForwardMovement.org. We are delighted to be doing this work and invite your prayers and support.